The Use of Self

The Use of Self
The Essence of Professional Education

Raymond Fox
Fordham University

LYCEUM
BOOKS, INC.

Chicago, Illinois

Copyright © 2011 by Lyceum Books, Inc.
Published by

LYCEUM BOOKS, INC.
5758 S. Blackstone Ave.
Chicago, Illinois 60637
773 + 643-1903 (Fax)
773 + 643-1902 (Phone)
lyceum@lyceumbooks.com
http://www.lyceumbooks.com

6   5   43   2   1   11   12   13   14   15

ISBN 978-1-933478-45-6
Printed in the United States of America

Library of Congress Cataloging-in-Publication Data

Fox, Raymond.
    The use of self : the essence of professional education / Raymond Fox.
        p.   cm.
    Includes bibliographical references and index.
    ISBN 978-1-933478-45-6 (pbk. : alk. paper)
    1. Teachers—Training of.   2. Teacher-student relationships.   3. Reflective teaching.   I. Title.
LB1707.F69   2011
370.71'1—dc22

                                                                2010039009

With gratitude, respect, and admiration for Tom, my son

who spurred me on and straightened me out—
with gentleness and intelligence,
with discipline and humor

who edited with originality and precision and great patience

who perhaps has taught me more than I ever taught him

who continues to teach me . . .

Contents

Preface

This book is the result of thirty-plus years in the classroom and equal time thinking and writing about teaching. I have come to the conclusion that we teach students much about science but little about caring and the art inherent in practice. The basis of much of our existing professional education is still promulgated through an outmoded model of lecture and textbook and memorization. It neither respects the individuality of those we teach nor mirrors the world in which we live, where mere facts and information mutate in an instant. Change is required. We need to make education more relevant, relational, and reflective.

Professional education, as well as professional practice, involves a deliberate, conscious, and disciplined use of self. Your *self* as teacher and as practitioner is the medium of transmission. The essential constituent of all professional encounters is self, composed of personality, knowledge, values, skills, and culture.

The optimal teacher and the optimal practitioner display strengths in both rational systemization and empathy. This allows them to render precise assessment and effective intervention as they make others feel heard, understood, and cared about. *The Use of Self: The Essence of Professional Education* posits that the rudiments of the professional encounter between teacher and student should substantially model ones that students are encouraged to employ with clients. As you reinforce students' practice efforts through knowledge-building, be aware that their reactions, thoughts, and feelings are equally integral to their learning.

It is therefore incumbent upon you, the teacher, to create the conditions that encourage mutuality, engagement, and active problem-solving, the same conditions that students are expected to provide for their clients.

I hold fast to the belief that students learn best how to respond to clients when we and they participate in a forum that is steady, safe, and consistent. Instruct students in what they need to know conceptually. Build a milieu conducive to honest, intensive, and meaningful interaction. Long-practiced skills and a deep understanding of your subject matter allow you to nurture and extend such an atmosphere.

The overall message of the book is for you to be accessible to students. Allow them to influence your procedures and policies. Offer choice. Provide variety. Establish and sustain an ambiance of sharing, openness, challenge, and change. Your power and authority as a teacher derive from the human qualities you evidence and the care with which you exemplify the curriculum's core messages. In this educational paradigm, skills, clinical decision-making, and respect for students and clients dominate. Your role is to mold students into scientifically sophisticated as well as humane, client-centered practitioners with a knowledge base grounded in discipline and a skill base anchored in art and compassion.

I believe that developing in students a sound practitioner sense is the goal. Textbooks make scant reference to such an endeavor. Knowledge can enhance this sense but it goes beyond knowledge. It as an elusive quality, not clearly defined, yet invaluable when it is present and noticeable when it is absent.

Acknowledgments

So much to be thankful for, so many to whom I am indebted. To name but a few:

I am grateful for my wife, Jeri, my tough critic and staunch supporter, for her helpful suggestions on this manuscript, but mostly for her enduring tolerance, encouragement, consolation, and love.

I am indebted to scores of students from whom the general ideas expressed in this book have been generated. It is a synthesis of their influence that has shaped, reformed, and refined my underlying philosophy and approach to teaching.

And to my forgiving and giving children, Tracy and Tom, whose sensitivity, continued interest, and constant affirmation stimulate these seemingly neverending writing ventures.

PART I
Basic Principles

For too long we have dismissed the subjective as ephemeral and of little consequence; as a result we have lost our center and been magnetically drawn to the shallow harbors and arid beaches of unrelieved objectivity.

—JAMES BUGENTAL

BUGENTAL ALLUDES TO the basic premise of this book—the intersection of *self* with *other* as the heart of both professional education and practice. It has three underlying themes—the centrality of presence, the impact of modeling, and the significance of reflection.

Part I of this book comprises five chapters: (1) Introduction; (2) Musings about Teaching and Learning; (3) Personal Presence and the Safe Class; (4) The Matrix of Modeling, Mentoring, and Mirroring; and (5) Reflection and Self-awareness. They embody the overarching philosophy that *relationship* and *reflection* are the basic building blocks of professional education.

These interconnected chapters integrate conceptual knowledge with affective and experiential processes. They focus on artistry and creativity. Emphasis is placed on the congruence between what happens in the class-room and what happens in the practitioner's office, and on the proposition that learning is promoted by an ongoing, dynamic, interdependent interplay between the teacher and students.

Effective teaching, as effective practice, entails self-awareness combined with the ability to build and sustain relationships conducive to change. In a climate of safety, you and your students cultivate a reciprocal and mutually influencing partnership. Purposeful and mindful dialogue advances students' appreciation of the student-client relationship and the ways to nurture it.

Stated more emphatically, these chapters advance the conviction that a strong parallel exists between the teacher-student and student-client relationship. Students witness firsthand your ability to show understanding and responsiveness. They learn the rudiments of professional helping when you treat them in ways substantially similar to the ways you teach them to treat clients.

The entire professional education process entails observation, imitation, and identification by students of your expertise. You model how to set goals, survey reactions, check atmosphere, tune-in, and induce change. As a model and mentor, you stimulate knowledge acquisition, offer sage counsel, serve as a sounding board, instruct students in technical skills, and provide support. You socialize them to professional role requirements, challenge them to self-examine, and construct a context in which new meaning can be discovered.

Intensive reflection overarches all else. It involves scrutinizing your actions—what, how, and, most important, *why* you do what you do. It entails honest discernment, which ultimately undergirds professional discretion.

Introduction

Good teaching is an act of generosity, a whim of the wanton muse, a craft that may grow with practice, and always risky business. It is, so to speak plainly, a maddening mystery.

—PARKER PALMER

While certainly a mystery, as Palmer suggests, a teacher's mission, as well as reward, is educating, drawing out from students what lies dormant while proposing the new, the exhilarating, the as-yet undiscovered.

WHY THIS BOOK?

Professors, especially those new to academe, frequently find themselves in the classroom with little preparation, guidance, or direction about *how* to convey the knowledge and skill set of the profession. The prevailing assumption is that advanced knowledge of subject matter itself is sufficient preparation to teach the subject. The unofficial credential for teaching is completion of a research doctorate in a particular discipline. This narrow position is reinforced by the belief that students will learn from a one-way transmission of information.

Many of us have learned to teach the hard way, by the seat of our pants, by circumstance, or by necessity. We often teach unaware of how we teach, both at the surface level of recognizing and identifying *what* we do in the classroom, and at the philosophical level of considering *why* we do what we do. Theoretical frameworks and findings from research studies provide only limited assistance in mastering the art and craft of teaching. Between the ideas that research provides and the kinds of direction and decisions you, the teacher, must make, there is a gulf.

3

Teachers, both new and experienced, seek practical yet innovative suggestions for creatively working with students. They need help with difficult
questions. How do I divide my focus between establishing a relationship,
developing a learning contract, and plunging into content? How can I enhance
the learning process without actually getting in the way? How do I best connect with students? How can I make learning active? In what ways can I per-
sonalize the teaching/learning environment? How do I adapt the method of
teaching to students' differing learning styles? How do I keep content fresh for
them and for me? How do I create a climate that is calming while challenging?
How do I build a secure place to invite learning and change?

OVERARCHING THEMES

Themes in this book resemble those in my other books that concentrate on
clinical practice. They are heartfelt and basic. Because there is a limited number of foundation premises that influence practice, and by extension, teaching, these are spotlighted because they form the basis for my personal and
professional life. While denotatively teaching refers to the transmission of
acquired knowledge, its connotative corollaries are of greater interest. What
are they? Relationship. Reflection. Self-awareness. Safety. Transparency. Modeling. Mentoring. Mirroring. And methods that support them.

The crux of this book is to weave together the rational and conceptual
with the creative and intuitive. The role of teacher shifts from being a storehouse of knowledge to being an exemplar of practice.

Reflective teaching involves the appreciation of the central roles of experience, mindfulness, artistry, critical thinking, and compassion. It involves who
we are as well as what we do. It obliges you to be purposeful, open, sensitive,
flexible, student-oriented, and creative.

This book attempts to seriously and conscientiously fuse the academic
with the popular, to promote meaningful learning that is challenging yet fun
for students as well as for ourselves. That learning keeps our work fresh and
exposes students to the uncertainties and complexities of practice.

Teasing out and capturing ideas about teaching for this book has itself
been an avenue for self-reflection. It has allowed for a personalized integration
of anecdote, scholarship, and speculation.

Perspective plays an important role in understanding ourselves as teachers. Without perspective, the discrete themes resemble a list of ingredients
that provide a sense of a completed dish but do not quite convey what it
tastes like. It helps to step outside of ourselves to examine our attitudes and
personal values about the teaching process, as well as the underlying assumptions and principles about learning that guide and direct our approach. Of
course, this process of self-examination is never complete. Every time we discover something new about theory, about learning, about students, about ourselves, there will still be other pieces of which we are unaware.

In honoring relationship and reflection, this book calls upon varied methodologies in a separate section—intensive journaling, storytelling, case study, role playing, and so on—that support these two emphases. It integrates conceptual knowledge—rational awareness and analytical thinking—yet places more emphasis on relational and experiential processes, intuition and artistry, interpretative ability, insight, and critical reflection.

Priority is given to creativity rather than routinization, cooperation rather than competition. The book suggests ways to invigorate yourself as you stimulate students. It offers strategies but, more important, appeals for supportive reflection, mindfulness, modeling, mentoring, and mirroring.

The book shifts away from promoting the dominant didactic form of content delivery. Though informed by science and theory, as well as extensive reading in the literature, it relies heavily on the experiential.

I believe that getting as close as possible to the subjective experience is at the core of professional practice and teaching. This position is based on the idea of influence—the behavior of one person affects the behavior of another. What students observe most closely, explore most intensely, and imagine most vividly are the faculty around them. There are no perfect theories, models, formulas. We teach by being present fully as ourselves and paying attention and interacting with students naturally to promote their full development as persons and as professionals.

Learning to be professional is not a purely intellectual endeavor. True, students need to learn to think in certain ways; they also need to perform particular skills and to practice in ways consistent with values, culture, and standards. These skills are mastered not by reading texts or listening to lectures, although these are relevant. If a picture is worth a thousand words, we must *show* our students a picture of teaching. Show them, don't just tell them. Do what I do as well as what I say.

In this book, I encourage a less rigid and more fluid and personal approach to teaching, an approach that opens the way to respond appropriately, differentially, and effectively to a wide range of students with a broad array of learning styles and experience.

Using an informal tone, I speak directly to you rather than addressing an anonymous teacher. This style reflects my bias about what I believe teaching can be.

THE TEACHER/PRACTITIONER

The Use of Self focuses on the elements of teaching and practice. It relates both to classroom and field instruction. References are made to a few selected theoretical concepts and formulations, but only insofar as they illuminate practical and useful teaching interventions.

Teaching and practice are isomorphs: both intend to promote change in thinking, feeling, and behavior by means of knowledge enhancement, example, analogy, and experience. There is a strong congruence between what happens in the classroom and what happens in the practitioner's office. They inform and resonate with each other. Professional education fails if it treats them as separate entities, which then leads to unimaginative teachers, ill-prepared student/practitioners, and—ultimately—underserved clients.

In short, the teacher-student relationship and the student-client relationship uncannily mirror each other.

Practitioners do not learn from the book. They function in indeterminate zones, involving value conflict and uncertainty. They rely on discretion and improvisation, constantly "inventing and testing in the situation strategies" of their devising (Schon, 1987, p. 5). You, through relationship-building, modeling, mentoring, and mirroring, can best prepare the student/practitioner for functioning in these indeterminate zones.

What happens in the classroom resembles what happens in the practitioner's office. The artistry of the student in the field reflects that of the teacher in the classroom. That artistry depends on conditions that encourage "freedom to learn by doing in a setting relatively low in risk, with access to coaches who initiate students into the 'traditions of the calling' and help them, by 'the right kind of telling,' to see on their own behalf and in their own way what they need most to see" (Schon, 1987, p. 17). Good teaching entails self-awareness combined with the ability to build and sustain relationships conducive to learning and artful methodology upon which both instructors and students can deeply reflect.

The classroom is a forum in which students read messages about practice in the teacher's and students' interchange. The degree to which teacher and students recognize and explicitly examine these messages determines the success or effectiveness of the educational endeavor.

REFLECTIVE TEACHING

The process of instruction and the content of the subject matter, especially in educating professionals who are expected to apply such knowledge in real-life encounters, should go hand in hand. Strain arises when teachers know content but little about how to convey it. One must give thoughtful attention to what one *does* in the classroom and *why* one does it. While good teaching requires command of the discipline, it also demands a conscious and deliberate consideration of self, relationship-building, reflective processes, students' learning patterns, imaginative delivery, and establishing a safe environment conducive to learning.

Schon argues that central to professional education are the concepts of "knowing-in-action, reflection-in-action, and reflection on reflection-in-action" (1987, p. 1). Reflection-in-action is a process-based framework where the teacher/practitioner and students come to understand themselves and their actions through the interplay between what they learn to do and what they actually do. Ultimately, what students learn within the classroom from the way you deliver content, engage them, and then reflect upon the whys and hows of your conduct, makes learning more immediately transferable to students' transactions with their clients.

Professional education differs from the humanities and sciences in that it relies equally as heavily on affect and values and, yet, is more inductive. Most important, it emphasizes the *application* of skills with consciousness and discipline. Specialized knowledge is necessary but not sufficient to prepare students for professional practice. It includes, but moves well beyond, presenting the theoretical, empirical research and evidence-based foundations of helping.

Teachers enrich content by encouraging students to assume an active role and a greater responsibility for their learning. Both teachers and students must reflect upon the meaning and significance of what they study through continual discerning dialogue.

A central ingredient involves students observing you deal with case and textual material and with theoretical content. This invites penetrating and alternative ways of thinking and responding. An even more critical component occurs as the students observe the teacher's conduct, the way you interact with individual students and the collective body of students, in the classroom as well as in informal conditions. When words match actions, you, the expert, are seen in engagement and intervention modeling the skills novices are expected either to consider adopting or adapting in their own performance with clients.

In the classroom, you display ways of working professionally. Students learn from the way you demonstrate your expertise in their presence. Such modeling gains greater power when you articulate and explain what and why you are doing as you do it. In this way you make visible and explicit as it happens how an expert appraises and approaches situations—tuning-in, contracting, goal-setting, assessing, negotiating, and so on. You demonstrate in vivo the interdependence of mindfulness, modeling, mentoring, and mirroring translated into active methods.

THE MARRIAGE OF CONTENT AND PROCESS, DISCIPLINE AND INSTRUCTION

Learning can occur without teaching. Teaching can occur without learning. Strain is created when instructors know content but know little about how to convey it. They neglect to appreciate that in educating for professional practice, the way content is delivered is as important as the content itself.

Keep in mind that the best we do for students en route to forming a professional identity is being professional ourselves. And what is being professional? It is grasping unique patterns in situations; absorbing vast amounts of information; integrating and critically assessing theory and research; discerning essential themes; being conscious, conscientious, and disciplined; and being aware of the impact of self. How do we proceed? Bruner (1996) writes that "the process includes conversation plus show-and-tell plus brooding on it all on one's own" (p. 116).

AFTERTHOUGHT

The Use of Self focuses on how to teach rather than on what to teach. This is a deliberate choice. In a broad sense, the professional and practice literature already concentrate largely on a dominant scientific and empirical tradition, on *content*. I endeavor here to balance this emphasis by highlighting the artistic and humanistic dimension of teaching, on *process*. The knowledge base of practice is crucial; the creative no less so.

The academy, as well as students and other faculty, clearly expect that you demonstrate proficiency in hard evidence of subject expertise. Tenure and promotion decisions require it. Student evaluation instruments seek to measure it. In the same vein, however, both the academy and students especially expect confirmation of "soft" constituents in the mastery of teaching. These include ways beyond telling or imposing correct viewpoints. They instead promote ways to involve and excite students in the educational endeavor—innovation, originality, engagement, enthusiasm, freshness. As well, they stimulate students' co-constructing and shaping their learning through critical thinking and challenging and critiquing what is presented.

This book appeals for your having an open mind in approaching your teaching, for appreciating the complexity inherent in professional education and practice, which entails so much more than the command of facts, figures, and findings. It asks you to think through the whys beyond the how-tos. It seeks to claim an equal voice and visible place for *delivery* in the entire professional education for practice enterprise.

While direct practice is its focal point, this book's message about teaching is applicable to all curriculum areas—human behavior, policy, and research. This focus devolves from my own real-world-practice background, augmented by a strong philosophical penchant. This penchant espouses that working with human dynamics competently requires more than an informed aptitude and technical skill. It requires profound consideration of the complex depth of the human equation. This book proposes ways to combine a technical accent with a discerning, conscious, and purposeful involvement with the subject matter and even moreso with students.

To ensure that teaching is commensurate with underlying ethical mandates and professional standards, I invite you to consider giving equivalent attention to the ideas presented about the nexus of content and process. Doing so anchors the foundational theoretical and research base of our profession with the artistic and humane. The intensity of the professional learning situation is an outgrowth of the exquisite blend of knowledge acquisition combined with your sharing openly your own personal stamp on it.

Musings about Teaching and Learning

> *Why is it, in spite of the fact that teaching by pouring in, learning by a passive absorption, are universally condemned, that they are still so entrenched in practice? That education is not an affair of "telling" and being told, but an active and constructive process, as a principle almost as generally violated in practice as conceded in theory.*

> —JOHN DEWEY

This book underscores two deep-seated convictions about teaching. The first abandons the idea that learning simply amounts to filling students' blank minds with missing supplies of theories, perspectives, statistics, and research reports. The second accepts the ideas that personal presence is the sine qua non of both professional practice and professional education.

Learning necessarily involves action and interaction. You, your students, and the context produced by your exchange is crucial. The single most important catalyst in this matrix is you—your self. Your personhood affects this exchange in a most significant way. Flowing from this overarching conviction are yet other intermingled building blocks of professional education. Among these are that professional education needs to be learner-focused, not content-centered; it needs to be active, collaborative, emotionally tinged, and tailored to students' styles.

In addition, professional education rests upon certain fundamental beliefs: learning accrues from facilitation; content and its conveyance should mesh; knowledge mastery is but one aspect of learning; thinking and feeling are inseparable; and effective teaching emanates from questioning, responding, and, most important of all, listening.

The chief vehicle for advancing professional education is initiating and sustaining a solid and positive relationship. Within a relational milieu, students feel free to examine assumptions, test values, share mistakes, experiment with alternative theories, try out new behaviors, and ultimately make strides toward professional development as self-aware, disciplined practitioners.

A BACKGROUND ACCOUNT

Teaching involves more than delivery. It stimulates discovery, elicits wonder. Your role mandates your understanding of how students learn and work, and your ability to enable them to draw upon your wisdom and talent as well as the resources you make available. It requires your finding out what they need to know and generating ways to convey it. Your challenge is to make your art so powerful that it appeals at the same time to the intellectual as well as to the emotional lives of students in a visceral way.

First-rate teaching looks effortless, maybe even easy. It is not. It appears as a seamless fabric when personal charisma and preparation synergistically unite. Take the occasion to inventory your strengths and style. Build upon them in the delivery of your knowledge and expertise. Consider an analogy, perhaps a forced one, between content (knowledge) and process (delivery) with a car and its driver. Science determines the car's basic composition; however, the art with which it is driven must be learned and practiced. Teaching necessarily relies on biological, psychological, and sociological knowledge bases but depends upon the art of your input to propel it forward.

BELIEFS ABOUT STUDENTS

A humanistic view, coupled with a strong dose of empathy, plays the most significant role in any professional endeavor, whether that be direct practice or teaching. An encounter in which the student is seen as a whole person through the lens of a person-to-person relationship underpins the particular success of the teacher-student encounter and, more generally, any helping process. To rephrase, in addition to learning from the detached objective abstraction of intellectually and conceptual sources, students learn from immediate and direct subjective experience of the relational and situational. This results in a deeper quality of professional understanding. You model and explicate what is implicit in these domains.

Some principles guiding my own teaching are that students learn best in a hands-on, inquiry-based manner; innately search for meaning; learn from images as well as from words; evolve from a world of past experience, which can and should be tapped; struggle to integrate previous experience with new learning; strive to participate in designing their learning; form their professional selves though interaction with you, other students, clients, and significant others; possess distinct and unique attributes and strengths; welcome challenge; progress in inexplicable circular spirals; seek mastery and respect; and exert great effort and endure considerable hardship to attain their aims.

Students need and are actively seeking alternative experiences, including opportunities to learn from teachers who offer diverse perspectives and innovative approaches. To learn to think critically, they also need to perceive that they have the opportunity to influence their own learning. Furthermore, they need to perceive that this learning is both plausible and transferable to their daily work. Active involvement gives them a special edge in being able to achieve autonomy as professionals.

Students come into their own when they have worked and reworked knowledge, put their mark on skill, imposed their own order on process, and adjusted it to fit with what they already possess.

You are a student yourself. You continually absorb new knowledge and experiment with new practice and teaching methods. As you do, assimilate them into your own developing style. Take seriously your own development and play an active part in genuinely collaborating with students to hone their own.

Students thrive when you provide conditions that support their goals and aspirations. When relationships are strong, when curriculum is rigorous and relevant, when opportunity to take ownership of learning is evident, students are more engaged, retain more knowledge, and more readily transfer what they learn to their work with clients.

BELIEFS ABOUT TEACHING

Teaching can be a messy affair. It is a painstaking, time-consuming job. It seeks to ensure that students are truly steeped in understanding and are not just parroting back abstract ideas or memorized facts by rote.

Itself a discipline with a scientific basis, teaching is a profession with its knowledge, skill, and value base. It is an exercise in action. It is, moreover, an art involving invention, preparation, and personal power. As such it appeals to emotion as well as to reason. It relies on interpersonal communication.

You have a significant impact on the learning process. Over the years, students have expressed the powerful message that they respond to human qualities that are displayed in the classroom and appreciate the teacher who provides more than simply information. Your openness, genuineness, and willingness to listen are critical variables in achieving educational goals.

You have your own charisma and your own expertise. How they are applied in your teaching depends on how you integrate them into your classroom repertoire and then how you conduct your own classes accordingly—with reflection, preparation, and flexibility.

Students should experience, firsthand from you, the interest, excitement, expertise, and, if it pertains, passion that you may expect them to deliver in their own practice with clients. Whether you intend it or not, students read subtle messages conveyed by your words but mostly by your gestures and tone about your competence as an expert. The nature and quality of your interaction, your purposeful and disciplined use of self is thereby a lesson in and of itself. Beyond didactic teaching is implicit learning: what students absorb and intercept from your nonverbal communication. Schon (1987) says it most emphatically: students experience and appreciate directly what is apprehended through absorption of what the teacher reflects verbally as well as nonverbally. He suggests that students learn from careful attention to the artistry with which you practice with them combined with your competence handling the material you present, and how honestly you critique it as well as yourself. This is particularly relevant in professional subject areas where uncertainty, uniqueness, and conflict abound. Your effectiveness as a teacher depends significantly upon the degree to which you and students recognize and explore mirrorings (the intermingling of modeling, mentoring, and mirroring investigated at length in chapter 3).

Students see if you, the expert, demonstrate in vivo what you instruct them, the novices, to do. Does your behavior match your words? Do you practice what you preach? Do you show yourself to be, by example, what you ask students to be? Are you truly excited? Are you invested in your subject? In them? If you are not groping, questioning, learning, and growing, what's the point? Why should they?

Paulo Freire (1970) suggests that teaching is a triadic structure of teacher, subject, and students. This perspective illuminates the connections between theoretical explanation, cultural and historical structures, and individual experience. He points out, echoing Schon (1987), that content is relatively fixed and stable. You and your students, on the other hand, are dynamic and fluid.

Continually evaluate your teaching and its impact on students. Remember, you are never just a teacher. You are a practitioner. You are an artist. You are a scientist. You are, consciously or unconsciously, an advocate of a point of view, a critic of certain positions, and, above all, an exemplar of clear communication, a seeker of meaning, a person devoted to the commonweal. You are a professional person entrusted with and responsible for others. Students wonder if they can trust and believe you if you do not exemplify these treasured attributes of a professional helper, if you are not with and for them.

You are an instrument for better and deeper understanding rather than merely a storehouse of knowledge. Your authority derives from your passion for the profession, for learning, for teaching, for reaching others. Take the time to figure out the most salubrious and effective ways to enliven content. Though there are no ready-made formulas for doing so, some ideas that may be helpful are explored in later chapters.

Be ready for teachable moments, *wow* moments—when you see the light bulb go on. These moments ignite both you and students with energy and excitement. They are unplanned. They are unpredictable, spontaneous, of uncertain provenance. Once they happen, allow them to flow. Relish these moments. If you have ordered your thoughts, prepared your notes, and selected your methods, you'll be able to temporarily suspend your agenda and capitalize on these surprisingly revealing moments, as well as connect them to course syllabi and goals. Doing so offers no certain guarantees either that learning will be elucidated or catapulted. If honored, nourished, exploited, however, it will release students' energy and enthusiasm. Recruit their energy and enthusiasm and direct it toward the object of the lesson. *Wow*, however, is not sufficient. When it occurs, welcome it, but amplify it.

Contrasting elements and theories, when taken together, may add rather than subtract from each other and provide a balance tailored to the specific needs of diverse students. Indeed, it is difficult to garner similar ideas unless their differences are highlighted. Instead of allegiance to one single approach, parts of many are combined in producing the most potent regimen for learning. Students should become familiar with a broad spectrum of theories, methods, techniques, and strategies for practice with individuals, families, and groups. Overall, be accessible to students, allow them input into courses and procedures, provide variety, and create a welcoming and safe atmosphere.

BELIEFS ABOUT LEARNING

For certain, your personal presence, creativity, and artistry are critical elements in professional education in an environment increasingly dominated by technology. Effective learning, though situational and variable, transcends electronic contrivances. It involves a linkage between intellectual activity and emotional involvement facilitated by face-to-face contact.

A vast amount of learning occurs though indirect, nonverbal means. As a result, the best teaching employs indirect, nonverbal methods as well as direct ones. This often means that the content of a lesson is less than clear-cut. This is a frustration at times, a blessing at others. Mastery goes well beyond memorization and counts for so much more. Groping toward *understanding* is equally as important, if not more important, than achieving knowledge.

Content and process are not contradictory. They are complementary, interdependent, and interlocking variables. When your class is working well, content and process are a seamless whole; it is neither necessary nor possible to distinguish one from the other. The *how* of the lesson and the *what* of the lesson interweave.

Get students inside a subject as well as get the subject inside the student. When students own the material, it sinks in. They cannot own it unless they participate in designing it, put their stamp or brand on it, alter it to fit with what they already have experienced.

Initially, students usually resent their opinions and beliefs being challenged. They prefer not to be disturbed and unsettled. Who doesn't? This inertia reflects a natural human characteristic—resistance to change. It often translates into questions like, "What do you want on the paper?" or, "What exactly should we review for the exam?" As if professional development involved something akin to solving a crossword puzzle. It doesn't. It is rather like engaging in a strenuous new course of physical exercise to reshape one's body. It entails missteps, mistakes, threats to long-accepted routines, feelings of ignorance, awkwardness, and uncertainty. Confront these resistances. Provoke and expand intellectual and affective horizons. Keep students alert and vigilant.

Make your transactions active. Offer students a fork to dig into new and challenging material rather than spoon-feeding them. Active dialogue with students bridges any chasm between you, the independent authority, and them, the dependent receptacle. It institutes a classroom resembling a research laboratory for integrating new knowledge while recreating and refashioning old knowledge into novel and exciting forms.

Have at your command versatility in techniques to spark students' interests. Variety is the spice of teaching. It keeps you and them awake and alert.

Recall teachers from your own background. Do you remember them for what they knew? What they said? You've probably forgotten. But you likely remember the stories they told, their unique ways of commanding your attention, their mannerisms and expressions. How did they affect you? How effective were they? Why or why not? Did you feel heard, understood? Do you remember those who were spellbinding? Those with whom you struggled to keep your eyes open? Those who transmitted original ideas? Those whose descriptions were colorful? Those who dogmatically adhered to one position? Those who merely read from the proverbial old yellow lecture notes? Those who sent you home with extensive reading and then gave you a pop quiz the next day?

Remember being their student, and think about how you might have delivered the lessons in the same or different ways. Would you have wanted the lessons to slow down? For there to be more time for assignment preparation? Time to figure things out and not just memorize or regurgitate information?

Wanting to be shown how to? Wanting a connection between what happened in class and what the book said and, ultimately, what you were supposed to do with clients? Wanting support and praise? And most of all wanting relationship. Take this sameness or differentness as a guide for yourself, as a starting point. Avoid what you objected to. Emulate what enlightened and enchanted you. *The way you were taught does not have to be the way you teach.* Try unconventional, innovative methods. You were probably drawn to your teachers' personhood before it dawned on you that they were scholars.

Personal Presence and the Safe Class

There is growing recognition among educators that, within a professional school, the individual and collective teaching, helping, and administering relationship with the student is the core of his preparation for professional relationship.

—CHARLOTTE TOWLE

Martin Buber decried the preponderance of I-it relationships, believing that they threatened human well-being. Thingification was the culprit. As we move further afield from everyday person-to-person experience, the special connection involving attentiveness, shared rapport, and synchronized verbal and nonverbal communication—in other words, *relationship* needs to be pursued and reclaimed. At the same time, drawing upon the work of D. W. Winnicott, creating and maintaining an environment for learning, by serving as a container for the anxiety associated with seeking new and unfamiliar knowledge, is a teacher's vital role.

There is a profound and pervasive relational dimension to teaching, especially teaching in the professions. The relationship is a unique and special one with identifiable similarities to the practitioner-client relationship. Both are based on the dynamics of human development and change. The mantle of professional authority derives partly from the intellectual, but more substantially through the immediacy, openness, and intimacy between you and students. The central passageway for you to help students learn the ground rules for practice—how to establish and sustain a relationship, to attend to another person, to pace interventions, to converse, to tune into others and, most important, how to manage their own feelings while engaged with others—lies in your intense connection with students. The optimum pattern in practice as well as in teaching is having a balanced brain, one with strengths in both empathy and in substantive know-how. This balance is achieved through relationship.

17

Students bring with them habits and beliefs that previously worked for them but are not professionally functional. The foundation of competence does not arise from amassing new theories and factual knowledge but, rather, from absorbing and synthesizing them into a new, improved, and integrated whole established through your firsthand contact.

To develop students' level of professional expertise, you need to interact in a manner consistent with what theory and research you preach. The relationship is the medium, a potent emotional channel, through which depth learning occurs and professional identity is formulated.

Your relationship with students serves as an exemplar for the student-client relationship outside the classroom. In other words, students respond to a responsive interpersonal environment to fuel their development as professional helpers.

Writers in the educational sphere—Charlotte Towle (1945, 1954), Paulo Freire (1970), Carl Rogers (1961), Malcolm Knowles (1980, 1984), Thomas Dewey (1938, 1974), David Kolb (1984), and Donald Schon (1983, 1987)—emphasize the interchangeability and mutuality in the roles of teacher and learner where an atmosphere of mutual acceptance and trust is fostered. What is essential is a gentle, centered, conscious effort to be a visible model of the way to be with others.

In very important ways, teaching reflects the challenge of all human relationships—to understand and to accept others as they are and at the same time nurture further growth. The transmission of the qualities of empathy, honesty, caring, compassion, and sensitivity occurs through the relationship.

Through your relationship with them, students learn content, but more important, engage in a process that forms the foundation of professional interpersonal skills. When there is full activation of communication, when you and your students are fully engaged, the joining of minds is in full force. Clarity and authenticity ensue.

THE CORE OF RELATIONSHIP

Relationship is the gateway to effectiveness as a professional, a paradigm for—and an instrument of—instruction, especially when accompanied by continual reflection. It goes well beyond simple rapport. While it necessarily involves what some call *climate* or *environment*, it adds up to more than all combined. It includes presentation style, clarity, and enthusiasm, yet supersedes them. Teaching involves being present to students in ways that establish a form and meaning of its own, paralleling that of the student and client. From this encounter, students incorporate mental models of the helping process, thus erecting an essential scaffold for their professional practice.

INTERACTION

Relationship-building has three basic purposes: (1) to establish and maintain relationships that reduce anxieties and defensiveness in the learner and enable him or her to open up for learning; (2) to bring about learning and change; and (3) to ultimately provide a paradigm for students to draw upon in the formulation of their own professional and practice development.

It is from your example that students learn to function to their fullest capacity as disciplined and autonomous practitioners who have integrated the key dimensions and ethics of the profession. This requires your interacting with them in such a way as to actively demonstrate requisite skills and values. Your classroom is a laboratory for learning the rudiments of practice; students, therefore, should experience firsthand from you the interest, empathy, acceptance, freedom, and openness they are expected to provide for their clients.

The impact of your teaching resides in how well you use yourself, how adeptly you read students, and how competently you employ sensitivity to guide students in developing their own purposeful use of self. Making this happen requires your ability to model behavior, reflect attitude, and explore thinking and feeling.

DIMENSIONS OF THE TEACHING RELATIONSHIP

Full engagement invariably feels risky when you must choose to enter unfamiliar territory. This choice requires courage and entails uncertainty, but consider that this is exactly the experience of students in your class and of clients in therapy. Both cognitive and emotional capacities are engaged in this transaction, and an attempt is made to translate knowing into doing. In all these instances, students experience vis-à-vis you, the expert, dependency, autonomy, competitiveness, fears of criticism and failure, as well as responsiveness and pleasure at accomplishments. These are accompanied by anxiety, fear, and resistance to change. In both instances, you are prone to feelings such as authoritativeness, inflexibility, disapproval, being "right," overly self-referenced, or, on the other hand, being too uncritically nurturing, overlooking problems or issues, and doting, all of which, when unrecognized, interfere with learning. In teaching as in practice, these ways of being demand constant scrutiny.

By building and sustaining relationships, you help students to more fully understand and effectively use their selves to help clients understand and express themselves. You accomplish this by providing to them in the classroom an authentic experience of empathic resonance. You effectively offer a firsthand sense of the rich depth of the human mind, an appreciation of mindfulness, and a grasp of the power of the relationship itself.

LEVELS OF THE TEACHING RELATIONSHIP

Your effectiveness and success in teaching depends largely upon your demonstrated ability to initiate and sustain an alliance with students. Every encounter stimulates learning and awareness of well-considered ways of being with clients. Interactions with people shape the development of the mind, and students transform your interactions and characteristics into inner regulations so that what is internalized becomes part of their own professional modus operandi.

COGNITIVE LEARNING

At its most obvious and uncomplicated level, teaching involves intellectual learning and didactic instruction. Its object is knowledge enhancement. At this level you appeal to the cognitive and conscious processes within students. You involve students in a dialogue in which they become aware of theory, research, and ideas. Together you explore the various options for understanding theoretical perspectives, examining research related to the evidence base of practice, and applying differential interventions in their work with clients.

Provide an explanation of exactly what is expected of them in practice situations. Approach the class with clear purpose, clarity, enthusiasm, and rigor. Endeavor to offer information in non-technical terms, and pace it to students' levels of experience. Direct and realistic critiquing of students' ongoing work and projects is paramount. This level of intellectual learning nourishes their sense of mastery over the rational and tangible aspects of the professional venture. In your role of didactic teacher, also provide technical assistance for developing and improving skills and assisting students to recognize their impact on clients. This is achieved when you thoughtfully review journals, ask key questions, provide challenging and new experiences, highlight inconsistencies, suggest modifications and alternatives, propose a variation of theoretical formulations, reframe, and focus.

Encourage students to read, research, and to confer with available experts. Learning is not restricted to material arising from textbooks. Contacting experts adds to dynamic understanding

Intellectual understanding is an essential ingredient in the educational enterprise. It bolsters knowledge and skill while focusing on increased ability to conceptualize the entire helping endeavor. It also underscores the empirical base for the helping process.

Although there are many approaches to developing these skills, active discourse is, as Towle (1954) suggests, the best means for cultivating critical thinking. While intellectual stimulation and mastery is clearly a necessary component in professional education, it is not sufficient.

INTERNALIZATION

Internalization arises from mutual reflection on your dyadic exchange and how you handle the dynamics of your encounter with the class as a whole as well as with individual students. Students are keenly attuned to your genuineness as a person and authenticity as a teacher and practitioner.

No matter how objective or intellectually focused you remain, there is an inevitable identification with you by students through their close observation.

Initially you provide direction in how to observe, how to question the taken-for-granted, and how to assess and frame new understanding. Because they have watched you doing so yourself, over time, students begin themselves to observe and come to question the meaning of their own experience, to reevaluate and reformulate their views, ideas, beliefs, values, and biases. Consequently, they formulate new meanings and try out new strategies.

Endeavor to reduce anxiety and convey an atmosphere of openness. Take an accurate pulse of the class. Students who feel off balance because of a critical attitude will have a poor experience and will likely resist learning. When the atmosphere is good enough, students feel free to examine or question the tenets you advance. Invite them to share their reflections and introspections about reading, research, experiments, writing and, more important, about your immediate association. Ask students to experience, examine, and ultimately talk about the problems, strains, and tensions as well as the ease and candor arising in the classroom with you, other students, content, and readings. Open discussion creates an atmosphere of mutuality and collegiality, more specifically, partnership in learning. It promotes reflection and discussion about the meaning and the mechanics in the establishment and maintenance of the teacher and student relationship and, by extension, the student and client relationship. Through this type of dialogue you assist students to liberate themselves from formulaic responses that limit their genuine involvement with each other, with you, and, ultimately, with their clients. Building a warm, supportive environment with a sense of security leads them to an alliance that eventually permits the expression of their doubts and apprehensions without fear of harsh judgment. It also moves toward advancement of a safe class.

No significant human relationship proceeds without conflict, stress, and stalemates. So, too, it is in the classroom. Moderate these. Tolerate and examine them to augment an overall harmonious functioning of the relationship.

Encourage mutuality and reciprocity so that barriers become foci for examination and represent interactive practice as it should operate in the client situation.

This process of internalization involves the way in which you establish an alliance, stay optimally in touch with the nature of students' experience, and handle their vulnerability within it. It pertains to the care you take in monitoring and selectively addressing their cues about confusion and anxiety in their own interaction with each other, with content, and with you. Students are exquisitely sensitive to your empathic resonance, your response to their subjective experience, and the way you convey understanding of their prejudices, feelings, attitudes, and ideas. Students identify with what they intuit about the elegance and refinement of your skills, while likely noting any clumsiness and imprudence—which, ideally, you have acknowledged and encouraged them to avoid. Internalization then involves students experiencing, taking in, or soaking up the manner in which you display empathy toward them and establish the core conditions for learning and for change.

Rogers (1958) describes these conditions—congruence, empathy, and unconditional positive regard. Students absorb and identify with your delicate and immediate facility in modeling them both in your ongoing exchange and in your comfort with such sensitive matters as dependence, conflict, and power. Students learn about empathy and the art of holding from being held, by feeling understood and heard, and learn how to transfer this learning to work with their own clients.

Students are attentive to your being able to engage in a deep interpersonal relationship without losing integrity or autonomy. They wonder, *Do you emerge as a genuine and caring person? Are you sufficiently integrated and free of your own stuff to be available to me? Do you exhibit the sensitivity, know-how, and insight you require of me to transfer to my daily work?*

INDEPENDENCE/MASTERY

When you flexibly interact with students, you encourage, recognize, and reinforce their facing and mastering difficult stresses of client interaction increasingly on their own. Their independence flourishes. Share personal experiences, admit uncertainties, accept new ideas, tolerate different opinions. As a result of your reliability, consistency, and emotional resonance, students themselves begin to assume those same attributes.

As they develop autonomy, students feel empowered to disagree with expert opinions and to offer their own countering views. They begin to trust yet scrutinize their subjective responses to the material and to rely on their own capacity to reflect on and think about their experience and trust their own self-analytic process.

KEEP IN MIND

The importance of the teacher-student relationship has been underestimated. It is a human relationship that is a unique construction created by the mutual interaction between teacher and students. Mutual engagement in building and maintaining this relationship is the key element for learning. It serves as the paradigm for students of the helping relationship. It is the vehicle through which essential knowledge is given, skill is developed, values are honed. More important, the very experiencing of the relationship itself is the essential learning experience. Emphasize the immediacy of your presence and attitudes, along with information, theory, research, or techniques. This special relationship enables students to enhance their observing ego and their capacity to integrate experiences into a meaningful system.

In terms of oneself, be aware, authentic, and attentive; maintain a sense of humor; remain sensitive to strengths, culture, and life space; support autonomy; acknowledge your own limitations and quirks; and be sincerely consistent in promoting direct, open dialogue. For students, provide a sense of fluid stability through revisable structure; nourish spontaneity, fascination, and curiosity; stimulate experimentation and self-revelation; invite feedback and act on it; recognize and celebrate accomplishments; offer choices; draw upon a range of experiential activities—videos, movies, role plays, cases; validate diverse perceptions and perspectives and be quick to address ruptures and dysfunctions.

THE SAFE CLASS

The wellspring of relationship-building is a "safe class," a facilitating and stable culture for learning. And the wellspring of a safe class is relationship-building. Relationship and safety are contemporaneous; they go hand in hand. The safe class is both a precursor and an outcome of the relationship.

Educational success involves myriad factors. Emotional elements such as motivation, persistence, and responsibility combine with sociological elements such as peer and group pressure. Likewise, patterns of learning and a trusting and open environment are crucial. The safe class offers the central passageway for you to help students learn the ground rules for practice—how to establish and sustain a relationship, to attend to another person, to pace interventions, to converse, to tune into others, and, very importantly, how to manage their own feelings while engaged with those of others. These tacit lessons lay the foundation for competent practice.

Rely upon sustaining a balance between challenge and support. This is accomplished when contact, connection, and access are maximized. Rogers

(1983) emphasizes creating such an environment, which he dubs "learner-centered." Your professional artistry in the classroom reflects that required of the student/practitioner. It depends on conditions you create to encourage "freedom to learn by doing in a setting relatively low in risk, with access to coaches who initiate students into the 'traditions of the calling' and help them, by 'the right kind of telling,' to see on their own behalf and in their own way what they need most to see" (Schon, 1987, p. 17).

Presence with others constitutes the lesson. Issues with which students grapple as they work with clients are issues that do not emanate exclusively from within people, but arise between people. In other words, people problems have their source in dysfunctional, harmful, inconsistent relationships. It follows then that learning to intervene to alter these problems requires being steeped oneself in an interpersonal milieu. The extent to which you facilitate students develop a more complex and coherent model of practice depends on your creating an atmosphere of safety wherein you provide the cues and opportunities for rigorous reflection.

Describing the safe class is elusive but approachable through four apparently paradoxical statements:

1. To be purposefully detached in a disciplined way requires first being attached.
2. To lose yourself in the mutually created classroom experience is to find yourself and discover new ideas and methods.
3. To be closely linked to others makes learning simultaneously risky and gripping.
4. The means is the end, the end is the means; in other words, process *is* outcome.

How is the safe class created? Offer a special and flexible space where the nature and quality of your interaction itself serves as a standard. Do it by being continually reliable and dependable, responding sensitively to students' reactions and questions, accepting them for who and where they are, yet urging them, non-judgmentally, to have a grasp of inner reality and interpersonal dynamics.

More specifically, you build a safe class by making yourself accessible to students, by actively offering assistance, by involving them in designing their plan for learning, not as a passive participant but as an active collaborator. A critical component involves being aware of what you bring into the process yourself.

Abandon a customary static approach. Enter the experience with students. Unfruitful learning results from rigid and distant interaction. Be highly visible as a facilitator of communication. Providing a safe class is prerequisite for open and effective work and serves as a basis for increasing knowledge, practicing new skills, altering perspectives, and tackling biases.

Be consistent and available. Be generous, receptive, and responsive. Show appreciation and patience. Create an ambiance of trust and support. Face students squarely. Show that you are present to them. Make your own reactions available for them to study. Impassivity cheats you and students of your most useful instrument—your own experience and ability to see and to share, and to reflect.

Building a safe class means opening a dialogue in which students witness firsthand your ability to show understanding and responsiveness. In a safe class, there is activity as well as reflection, doing as well as saying, looking outward as well as inward. Emphasis is placed on the human experience of an active, striving, affirming, and potentiating transaction, on recognizing the here and now.

If you cannot get yourself into the students' shoes, as it were, and somehow give them modeling as well as resources, little will be gained. Have your actions match your words. Talk the talk *and* walk the walk. Students progress when they experience your expertise as a practitioner in an immediate and intense way. Heinz Kohut writes: "I must now, unfortunately, add that empathy per se, the mere presence of empathy, has also a beneficial, in a broad sense, therapeutic effect—both in the clinical setting and in human life, in general" (1977, p. 85). The safe class is more than symbolic metaphor. When you involve yourself and participate fully with students, your experiential growth will match theirs.

EMPATHY

The technical name for your attunement to students in creating a safe class is *empathy*. You do not need to be perfect, but you do need to be sensitive enough to them. Demonstrate in vivo the capacity to project yourself into the experience of others—more particularly, into theirs. Empathy materializes when it is actually undergone.

Empathy is a mode of gathering information by attending to and conveying your own experience in the presence of students. It requires your ability to oscillate from observer to participant and back to observer. It allows you access to students' ongoing learning experience, and in doing so, moves you away from any tendency to view them simply as the repository of knowledge and information. It is an essential prerequisite for your ability to demonstrate a path toward voicing your understanding of your inner thoughts and feelings and behavior in such a way that students can absorb and understand. This feeling of understanding strengthens your alliance with them.

Empathy has the potential to bring the clarity of rational logic to bear upon the profundity of affective experience, a way to synthesize two apparently antithetical figures: your being a dispassionate and rational scientist (left brain) and your being an attuned resonating artist (right brain).

Providing a safe class, then, is metaphoric shorthand for being empathic.

The Matrix of Modeling, Mentoring, and Mirroring

How we learn is what we learn.

—BONNIE FRIEDMAN

The critical role of the teacher is laying the paradigmatic groundwork for students' learning to be professional. Teachers manifest in their comportment the intellectual, affective, and ethical bases of professional expertise. Their very conduct, enhanced by knowledge, embodies the essential message about how to be a helper.

Three interwoven processes—modeling, mentoring, and mirroring—form the basis for professional education. They are converging and commingling processes, not independent elements in learning, as described here for intelligibility's sake; they are multidirectional in influence and spiral back on each other, comprising a wholesome and fulfilling professional educational venture. Each individual mode is important in and of itself, but their interrelationship is the compelling element.

MODELING

Modeling is a complex process involving observation, imitation, and identification by students of the teacher. It occurs whether or not you intend it or not.

Many of the same skills and conditions that promote client growth promote student growth. Strive to create an ambiance that engages students. Seek to engross them at a level that allows them to take the concepts they learn, as well as the examples you provide, whether tacitly or explicitly, from seeing you practice with them in class, and transfer them to their contact with clients. The words you utter, the actions you take, the manner in which you conduct the class are carefully observed and considered by students. They attend to your preparation, enthusiasm, and relatedness as lived lessons about how to deliver these same attributes and functions with clients. They observe your unspoken feedback—how your tone and facial expression reveal whether you are attuned and on the right track.

In your interaction with students, whether consciously or not, you continually display your own competence in your discipline. Students observe how you practice what you preach in your dealings with them, with colleagues, with syllabus material, nascent ideas, and theories. They inevitably appraise your ability to facilitate communication, manage dilemmas, encourage mutuality, and foster cooperation in working associations with others. They assess your patience, availability, and skill. They learn mainly from the ongoing flow of feedback, from your tone, your facial expression, and the overall manner in which you exhibit your attunement with them. Students ask, "Do you demonstrate yourself to be the kind of practitioner that you expect me to be?" "Are you keenly attuned to timing; are you sensitive, aware of nuances?" "Do you identify and verbalize tension openly and deal with it?" "Are you credible as a professional and remain real as a person?" "Do you temper your authority?" "Do you stay in tune for the entire class period?" "Do you sustain your excitement?" "Are you open to fresh ideas?" In brief, "Should I be like you?" Characteristics you should be modeling include warmth, acceptance, respect, understanding, interest, tact, maturity, belief in your own ability, and generalized reinforcement.

BEING AN EFFECTIVE MODEL

Effective teachers model ways of doing work and articulate what they are doing. They explain *why* they do what they do. They help students to see them, their thinking, feeling, and values as they actively demonstrate the integration of knowledge in action. Be tolerant of students' different and even opposing viewpoints, prejudices, and beliefs; do not impose your own. Invite students to share their hesitations and disclose uncertainties or certainties; confront evasions of difficult and challenging material, and do not cut them off. In this way you make visible and explicit how an expert appraises and approaches clinical situations.

Setting goals, surveying reactions, checking atmosphere, tuning in, and providing examples are among the strategies, applicable to clients, that students absorb from you. To be successful in enabling them to internalize and to differentially employ knowledge and skills, display and elucidate, when possible, the processes you yourself rely on. What, more specifically, should you intentionally model? Certainly go beyond data to identify meaningful patterns in information; respond to context; address breaches in communication; regulate disruptive behavior.

Deal directly with uncertainties. Demonstrate expertise in defining issues as they evolve in the class, consider aloud appropriate interpretations, uncover complexities, identify the array of response options, advance alternative theoretical and empirical viewpoints, assess the potential impact of these options, articulate your biases and their impact, and consider the limitations of potential solutions. These classroom interactions form a paradigm that can be duplicated in practice situations with clients. When you frame your process by articulating your ideas and procedures, students intercept a clearer conception of what performance is expected of them. As you self-evaluate, you effectively draw students' attention to the expectation that they self-evaluate. You encourage students to look over their own performance by continually looking at and accounting for your own. How do you arrive at conclusions? What do you take into consideration when making a diagnosis? How do you plan strategies for intervention? How do you examine the impact of your own work?

An example of what I refer to as a "grid" paradigm for modeling occurs in a course on teaching. Doctoral candidates taking the class are inevitably concerned about classroom management. They wonder how to respond to students' verbal as well as nonverbal messages that are communicated through tone, facial expression, and body postures. To conceptualize the concept of management, the grid shown in table 1 is proposed, and students are asked to talk about classes they are engaged in teaching as adjuncts or our own class in terms of the following layout: selecting behaviors that they identify—for example, silence, fidgeting, cross talk—we consider the possible

Table 1. Classroom Management

Classroom Management			
Student Behavior	Possible Meaning of Behavior	Check It Out	Potential Interventions

meanings of that behavior and advise checking out with the students the possible explanation that you have and then identifying potential ways of addressing the troublesome behavior.

This paradigm emphasizes differential responses to what transpires in the classroom. There is no unitary way to deal with particular behaviors such as silence, yawning, eating, speaking on the cell phone, and so on. It does not focus on the behavior per se, but on attempting with a critical eye to fathom the possible explanations underpinning the behavior. Intervention is then designed to intervene in this specific context. The next step is to offer their suggestions for addressing it. Naturally, immediate or automatic reaction is not always possible in terms of acuity or time of reflection on the dynamics of the classroom. Take the occasion to journal about it soon after. Such journaling will augment your inferential ability and crystallize your experience.

Yet another model is the comparison of theoretical frameworks (see table 2). This particular model enhances participation and fosters the art of intelligent conversation about complex issues. It allows students to advance and support their positions or arguments as it encourages tolerance for different and conflicting ideas. It turns over to students a considerable amount of responsibility for learning while allowing for integration of an array of ideas. Interestingly, a bonus arises when novel and unique ways of thinking offer you ideas you may not have thought about. Students often advance pithy and straightforward analyses that capture ideas in a way that makes them more accessible and memorable for everyone in the room.

Table 2. Theoretical Frameworks

		Theoretical Frameworks		
	Theory A	Theory B	Theory C	Theory D
Goals				
Assumptions				
Principles				
Strategy				
Evaluation				

I draw upon a "split screen" technique that requires alternating between conducting a lesson, doing an exercise, or suggesting an experiment, and then stepping aside to examine its whys and wherefores. The weaving back and forth generates energy, excitement, and scrutiny.

Reflection is profoundly influenced by examination of ongoing interactions of the expert and novices. As the class unfolds, inform students of your instructional decisions and underlying theories that support your decisions along with the various possible alternatives. Fathom what automatically and intangibly feels right into concrete terms. In doing so, you model for students a structure to conceptualize experience and consider differing theoretical interpretations.

Stepping in and out of the act of teaching as it happens, commenting on what you are doing, and inviting students' feedback, you disclose your own thinking and reveal your own decision-making, your reflection in action.

Split-screening relies on putting into practice the information and knowledge at your command, an ability to analyze immediately the situation with which you are confronted, synthesizing the elements, and translating it as it occurs into action. In reflecting in action, you continually step in and out of teaching, inviting students to comment on what they see you doing, to advance ideas about its purpose and to identify the techniques you are employing. Students are challenged to observe, articulate their observations, and conceptualize the experience as it unfolds before them. Instruction is thereby split into two screens: one interacting directly with the class in a typical teaching role; and the other encouraging students to reflect on the interaction. The reflective position is heightened with such questions as: "What did we just do?" "What did you observe about our exchange?" "How did my interaction with you demonstrate the principle we have been studying?" "What values underlie the questions I am now asking you?" "Why do I offer you choice?" "What is the purpose in this exercise itself?" Piggyback on their comments to validate their perceptions and acknowledge points or methods you did not recognize yourself.

To create further reflection, reflection in action, you are challenged to be transparent in sharing your own perceptions, motivation, purpose, rationale, and decision-making for proceeding. "As I hear your question, I am torn between answering you directly, asking you a question in return, or inviting other students to respond to you." "How does my behavior mirror today's topic?" This juxtaposed split-screen interface challenges you and students to scrutinize, analyze, ponder, and enunciate your lived process.

Split-screening involves a continuous live delivery of content related to the teaching/learning interchange accompanied by instant replay and critique of the presentation in terms of focus, method, instructional material, alternative venues, and so on. In a way, it makes the invisible visible when subtle or hitherto ignored ideas, beliefs, and interventions are manifested and explicated. Whether focused on an assigned reading, a role play, an experiential technique, or in more proximate terms, your handling of student questions or behavior divulges your ideas about what is happening and why you believe it is happening, why you responded in a particular way, and what framework you are adopting at the moment.

A critical dimension of such split-screening requires you to pause to take stock in an array of ways that interactions are occurring immediately in front of you. When you are thinking aloud in the classroom about your teaching and choices, you clarify and explicate your philosophy, opinions, assumptions, and biases; explore multiple perspectives, explain your own actions, examine alternative approaches for yourself, and inevitably welcome students to do likewise. At the same time, in being transparent, you open the door for the formulation of new options and opportunity to play with a range of novel ideas. Consider bringing to the foreground more than verbal interactions. Explicate paralinguistic features and their impact and relevance to achieve mindfulness.

For example, contracting may be read about, didactically presented, and role-played, but when it actually occurs directly in the classroom as students and teacher negotiate a contract regarding assignments, due dates, format, and so on, it becomes a vital paradigm for integrating and understanding the process. Once again alluding to the previous example, our concurring as students and instructor about next steps and ways to proceed, then vocally committing to this agreement is, effectively, a lived instance of contracting.

The concept of mutuality is thereby more fully demonstrated and integrated. Other components of the helping endeavor (e.g., questioning, eliciting information, giving advice) can be similarly highlighted, creating in the classroom an encounter paralleling the one students face with clients.

BEYOND IMITATION

The notion of imitation is frequently disparaged, yet it is, nevertheless, instrumental in learning. Children learn to play by imitating others and learn to function by imitating those around them. This prototype pertains to adults as well. En route to becoming professionals, students learn new skills in part by imitating others, especially experts, who have command of knowledge and skill.

Your role, then, is that of model. Students apprehend and learn from your frankness about how you work or, when appropriate, about your own relevant personal experiences. They wonder, in effect, "Is this how I might handle a similar situation?" You are an example of practice excellence. For example, a student, Mr. J, was late for class the day we were covering existentialism. It was not the first time. He made it a point after class, as other students lingered to listen, to ask why I did not stare blankly or disapprovingly at him when he entered, as other professors did. It was a firsthand ownership issue: when he chose to be late, he chose to miss the material. It was his choice, and he needed to accept responsibility for his actions. Others in the room grasped the exchange was a lived experience totally in accord with the fundamentals of existentialism.

When you actively listen and use basic attending and facilitation skills, you provide a model of engagement for students to adopt or adapt in their interpersonal contact with clients. Much of this dimension of learning is implicit. Students witness your unspoken modeling. What is inherent in this dimension? Basically, you demonstrate an ability to be authentic, to self-reflect, to take stock of yourself. It is through this passive form of learning that they rehearse ways of practicing with clients.

Imitation is reinforced when you explicitly share with students how you are affected by their participation and inquire about your effect on them. "Is what I am saying clear?" "Is there another way of presenting the material?" "Should we devote more time to this case situation?" "What makes sense in terms of next steps?" You model a way of operating, without imposing a preset idea that things can only be done your way, which undoubtedly influences students' frameworks for practice.

SELF-REGULATION

A prominent feature of social learning theory is its emphasis on self-regulation. This depends largely on awareness of oneself. Students need to develop the capacity to anticipate the consequences of their own actions as well as other people's responses to these actions. Unlike some of the traditional psychological theories, social learning theory contends that students can learn by observing others' behavior as well as from direct experiences. It stresses the importance, therefore, of modeling.

Students create a mental representation of your practice with them. At firsthand, they see you display the prescribed standards of professional behavior in different situations. You portray the care, compassion, and sensitivity with them that characterizes any helping endeavor. Retained in this image are your ways of defining issues and situations, of interpreting them, of close examination and discussion of options with their advantages and limitations, the impact of these options, alternative perspectives, recognizing personal biases, and understanding the complexities and uncertainties; your genuineness as a person; your active listening and attending; your mastery in organizing knowledge around themes; your fluency with theory; your fluidity in interaction; your self-monitoring and self-correcting behavior; your exposing your limitations and vulnerability; your facility in providing feedback.

While learning occurs passively and implicitly, it gains power when it is active and manifest. Your mantle of authority is derived in part from the intellectual. It is in the larger part derived from your affective compact with students.

The bottom line: seeing is believing. You should evidence the ethical importance of transparency with your students. Show them how. Provide a rationale for what you do. As you deal with classes in a calm and methodological manner, students witness positive outcomes. When you are faithful to the principle of being an honest broker of knowledge and skill, students will absorb the message and attempt to become honest brokers themselves.

MENTORING

Educators from all disciplines struggle with how best to transmit knowledge and skill, to cultivate professional development of students, and to create environments that are conducive and supportive to actualizing their innate potential. These factors are central and pivotal ingredients in professional education. Mentoring crystallizes professional development by focusing on the integration of technical skills, knowledge, and personal values. It socializes students into professional life.

Mentoring involves a shared relationship in two distinct ways. You, the mentor, possess theoretical knowledge and practice expertise; the student has hands-on experience of what it is like to be in the room with a client. This intersection profits both of you.

Much in this section speaks ideally about mentors—and, granted, mentors have been known to ignore, exploit, misappropriate, and downright plagiarize those they mentor. If you have been lucky yourself, you have had mentors who took you under their wings and showed you the ropes. They took a special interest in you, sustaining you in tough times, keeping problems and goals in perspective. Most important, they provided an image of how to conduct yourself in the professional world.

Mentors perform a multitude of functions: stimulating the acquisition of knowledge; offering wise and friendly counsel; acting as a sounding board; training in the technical aspects of the profession; providing emotional support and encouragement during times of doubt or turmoil; socializing students to the role requirements, expectations, and imperatives of the profession; challenging them to face quandaries; constructing a context in which new meaning can be discovered; and validating growth. While the specific functions vary, mentoring cannot be defined by formal roles alone. It is distinguished, rather, by taking students under your wing. You accept and confirm them, validate them.

Sharing a narrative of your own journey toward attaining your credentials, for example, provides a map for students to visualize in initiating their own. In effect, you usher students into making a transition from being students to being qualified practitioners. You coax them along. The story of your own professional development can be instrumental in passing on the values and wisdom that helped you on your road toward success—hard work, risk-taking, respectfulness, questioning the status quo, setting goals, and taking meaningful action toward your accomplishment.

As a mentor, through cognitive and emotional convergence, you spark in students a desire for advancing professionally. It may manifest itself in a variety of ways. This variety, however, resembles the examples you set. You facilitate their transition from beginning novices to proficient masters.

It is generally accepted that learning takes place throughout life. Adults as well as children learn a great deal indirectly. They learn a great deal out of the classroom as well as in it. We learn from our families, our work, our friends, and from daily encounters. We learn from problems resolved and tasks achieved. We learn from dilemmas and challenges. And we learn the most patently from concerned, generous, conscientious, and sharing mentors.

Erik Erikson's theoretical model of the eight stages of man, specifically the seventh stage, generativity versus stagnation, refers to the evolutionary development of humans, the teaching as well as the learning animal. Generativity concerns establishing and guiding the next generation (Erikson, 1950). Mentors themselves often have had mentors. Here is an opportunity to give back. Pause for a moment to ponder your own professional development. Have you experienced individuals who steered you in the right direction? Did you see eye to eye? How do you regard them now in your memory? Do you recall how that relationship developed? Do you recollect the impact that it had on you? What were the major variables that cemented the relationship?

Mentoring is instrumental in promoting growth, inspiration, and celebration. It is generally undertaken with a single student but can be a small group of students as well. It is close and intimate as you, an experienced, seasoned counselor, usually of superior rank and special achievement, guide the intellectual, emotional, and professional growth of less experienced students. Partnership is an integral characteristic. One-to-one mentorship, particularly, enables individual students to expand skills, to learn about using their experiences as a basis for interactions, to listen more attentively, to deal with anxiety, and to develop patterns of response. Furthermore, when you mentor students, your special and distinctive interest sustains them when times get tough. It keeps problems in perspective, and, most valuable, models how to conduct oneself as a practitioner, a colleague, and a professional. A trusted tutor, you provide information, emotionally support and encourage, challenge, and propel students toward a continuing interest in the enterprises of learning and of practice.

This component of teaching more frequently than not concentrates on contact outside the regular classroom. When mentoring, you are in a more advantageous position to tailor learning to the more immediate and unique educational needs of individual students. You share your tricks of the trade through straight talk.

GROUP MENTORING

Mentoring, difficult though not impossible when undertaken with a collective of students, resembles team coaching in sports—giving guidance, hints, pep talks, and tips. In class, but more especially in small seminar settings, observing students carry out experiments, enact role plays, and approach assignments allows you to offer immediate feedback and commentary with reminders about how these help to achieve goals and influence practice with clients. You encourage them to bring their performance closer to an expert level and enable them to calibrate their own progress. Your charge is to be accurate, timely, accessible, and direct.

What you cannot convey in direct ways may nonetheless be absorbed by association. The way you manage your own and the students' complex mixture of roles, tasks, and emotions instructs them in ways to manage their own interaction with clients, colleagues, and fellow learners. More important, it impels them toward greater responsiveness and compassion in their own functioning. How you relate to them broadens their perspective of the helping process and deepens their view of how a professional helper behaves.

Tracking the process of change in this mutually influencing relationship shapes the organization of their professional selves. Some degree of identification coupled with imitation eventually leads to individuation in the process of professional development.

Growth in a true mentorship is neither exclusive nor one-sided. It is complementary. It attends to students but at the same time responds equally to your needs for recognition, being influential, making a difference. It reflects the belief that if true learning is to occur in a fully human manner, honest and deep encounter through dialogue must be present.

As a mentor you provide the opportunity for students to experience firsthand the support and guidance from someone independent of their family or peer system. Mentoring is especially instrumental and pivotal in helping students who are at a crossroads in their professional life. Often mentoring permits students from diverse backgrounds, who might not ordinarily come into contact with a wiser and more experienced person, to originate and sustain a meaningful specialized relationship.

A good fit and trust, combined with reciprocal and respectful communication, are vital ingredients. Exploring possibilities, setting goals, choosing activities, and mutually celebrating accomplishments are integral parts of the process. Accompanying this with the active navigation of differences, conflicts, and limitations—and the negotiation of ways to meet and surmount them—allows for the cycle to proceed at a deeper level.

Mentoring relationships can occur through every stage of personal and professional growth and development. The relationship constantly changes and evolves. One may have several mentors addressing specific needs. Some mentoring relationships are time-limited or can last a lifetime. Not all mentoring relationships progress smoothly; conflicts may be evident at any stage of the relationship. Based on the context of the relationship, mentors are generally senior, usually an authority. A mentoring relationship, as other working relationships, has a sense of devotion, a give-and-take quality, and outcomes that include an increased sense of self-awareness in both the mentor and protégé. When the relationship is a good fit and beneficial as experienced by the individuals, it creates a powerful interaction that promotes development.

In summary, good mentoring is like good parenting. It provides the necessary supports in very real and symbolic ways—values, knowledge, skills—and then fades into the background, leaving the one mentored enriched, stronger, and independent. Your reward is watching students prosper.

MIRRORING

Mirroring, a more difficult concept to elucidate than either modeling or mentoring, occurs at two levels. The first refers to your acknowledging students for *what they do*, affirming their accomplishments, approving their development as students and imminent qualified practitioners. The second refers to your awareness, creativity, and availability in validating students for *who they are*—meeting their need for understanding and acceptance as people. Some of these needs for validation and affirmation are met to a limited degree simply through accomplishment. You fulfill some of these needs through the process of mirroring. Knowledge, even self-knowledge, needs to be validated outside of the self.

Human functioning is embedded in social interactions. These interactions, as they relate to development in general and to the achievement and maintenance of self-confidence, are fulfilled by experiences and relationships with others. Thus, in the first mode, recognize the central importance of positive experiences facilitating the formation of a strong, autonomous, and cohesive character, the core of a professional self. This occurs as students intercept and integrate your expressed confidence in them, applaud their achievements, and offer constructive critiques. They see and respect your opinion of their aptitude. Such corroboration, one aspect of mirroring, reinforces their confidence and performance. Give a word of admiration, a compliment appreciating their work.

In the second mode, students, while in your presence, experience the subjective side of you, experience a sense of your personal qualities—warmth, acumen, inspired thinking. Making known your doubts, uncertainties, even fears gives them permission to contact and to expose their own. As a result of your own introspection and candor, you made an unexpressed expectation for them to do the same. Your certainty and confidence in your personhood is infused. Students, through your example, through this form of mirroring, develop an internal means to maintain esteem and confidence in the face of unavoidable mistakes and failures. At the same time, they come to accept the worth of what they do and of who they are. As students become more certain of themselves, they require less support from you and increasingly feel confident in their knowledge and skill and affirmed as selves. Mirroring lends them your self-structure on which to build their own inner regulation.

Why is this second dimension so difficult to illuminate? It is difficult to illuminate because it occurs at an unconscious level. Students sense how you overcome self-doubt, how you firm up the integration of your personal and professional self, and how you derive comfort and satisfaction from this unification in exercising your role as a professional helper. In brief, in addition to experiencing your trust, warmth, and empathy toward them, students experience your humanness, your personhood. They catch the character and care that you portray as a professional, and, more fundamentally, as a human being. They look into the way you draw upon your own internal resources to guide them into fathoming their own.

This sounds so vague, maybe even hokey; however, it is tough to offer a concrete illustration. Continually endeavor to commit yourself to self-awareness, to dedicate yourself to excellence in practice, to confirm your interest in knowledge transmittal, to listen intently to students, and arouse their interest and motivation. Students will intercept your sincere effort. Give them a peek at the authentic you. Admit uncertainties and mistakes. Seek. Do not ask them to do what you would not do yourself.

Students are constantly vigilant. They study how you engage in a deep interpersonal relationship with purpose and discipline, remain empathic, and show concern without compromising standards, and, in doing so, maintain integrity or autonomy. They wonder, "Are you a genuine and caring person?" "Are you sufficiently integrated and open to be available to me?"

The hallmark of modeling, mentoring, and mirroring is having the heart, the integrity, and the courage to be yourself, as you would have students themselves be.

Reflection and Self-awareness

Teachers must be actively committed to a process of self-actualization that promotes their own well-being if they are to teach in a manner that empowers students.

—BELL HOOKS

"Know thyself," advises Socrates. "To thine own self be true," recommends Shakespeare. Being cognizant of your attributes, limitations, and style heightens your ability to draw selectively upon your own resources and fuels students' strengths. It kindles expanding levels of awareness, competence, and confidence in all of you. Awareness of self as person, practitioner, and as teacher is critical.

Competencies distinguishing the best from the worst in the helping professions have little to do with theory and technical acumen. They have everything to do with emotional and social know-how. Such know-how is cultivated though an intensive reflective process, the cornerstone of which exceeds abstract theoretical or technical knowledge. Experience and tacit knowledge upon which you rely everyday, almost automatically, when raised to the conscious level, is even more important. As a teacher, reflection goes well beyond improving performance in one particular course. It concentrates as well on consideration about your teaching in general and awareness of your own reflective processes.

Practitioners, as well as teachers, include *understanding*, as contrasted with *explanation*, as essential to their work. Understanding entails the discipline of attending, noticing, and appreciating others as human subjects. It is very different from explaining and can emerge only gradually when it is tended and nurtured by reflection. Understanding transcends translating or reducing experience to interpretation. As you teach, engage the left hemisphere, chiefly responsible for explanation of data, in tandem with the right hemisphere, chiefly responsible for overall representation, to engender context-rich understanding.

All this is not to say that practitioners and teachers are not scientists and do not think critically, but rather that their unique stance concentrates on their heart as well as their head.

Talented practitioners think critically and systematically about client needs, practice tasks, and service outcomes. They possess the ability to incorporate knowledge and skills into their work. That is, they understand client behaviors and concerns, the forces and factors that affect clients' lives, and are able to select strategies and techniques appropriate to their clients' conditions. They can identify the conceptual frameworks and empirical bases guiding their work and, most important, can continuously monitor and evaluate their efforts to ensure that these are indeed working and are consistent with a value base undergirding their profession.

The ability to think about what they are doing and why they are doing it is at the heart of professional helping. In like fashion, especially in the caring professions, competent teachers think critically and systematically about student needs, tasks, and educational outcomes. Competence requires analysis of their knowledge and skill base, but it takes more than thinking. A truly reflective process deviates from strict reliance on empirical and educational theory to recognition that experience itself develops knowledge that can guide the actions of teachers as well as students.

The concept of reflection has been defined and described in different ways. It defies simple explanation. It has no formula. Thankfully, it is not prescriptive.

Reflection is a vehicle for manifesting experiential knowledge. It entails a greater awareness of self and of the nature and impact of your performance, thus leading to improved functioning. It does not ignore the relevance of formal knowledge, but is accretive. It entails examination of uncomfortable feelings and rigid thoughts, and a willingness to consider alternative perspectives.

BACKBONE PHILOSOPHIES

Six theoretical, educational, and philosophical authors, originating from an array of disciplines, put forward ideas advanced in this chapter and echoed throughout this book. Charlotte Towle, David Kolb, Thomas Dewey, Paulo Freire, Carl Rogers, and Donald Schon articulate principles and processes that inform the ways in which teachers can build upon students' potential and strength. Each one, in different ways, questions the relevance of a technical/rational approach to practice and to teaching. All highlight the importance of experience, intuition, imagination, relationship, and especially reflection as integral to practice and teaching.

Charlotte Towle

Towle (1954) proposed four principles regarding the student-teacher relationship. She recommended that teachers: (1) respond to the valid dependency brought by students to the learning process, recognize their limitations and failures, and assist them to gain competency; (2) affirm the strengths of students, employ methods to engage them in learning, place responsibility on them for class preparation, class discussion, and seeking help when needed; (3) avoid making unrealistic demands, acknowledging the students' place in the curriculum and avoiding projecting standards beyond their current capability; and (4) ensure that students meet realistic demands.

Towle regards the educational relationship as fostering a sense of professional identity for students as they observe the teacher, in ongoing interaction with them, display the types of thinking and doing that exemplify meeting the standards of professional demands. She advises against focusing exclusively on the *what* and *how* of doing. She cautions teachers not to overlook the *why* of thinking and doing, which she sees as so critical to the linkage and assimilation of knowledge and skill (1954).

To facilitate the integration of learning, Towle advocates a reduced reliance on didactic teaching and a greater use of methods and materials designed to engage the learner more actively in problem-solving activities. The body of knowledge should be conveyed through material of increasing depth and complexity, written assignments, case records, books, and journals. All aid in the personal recollection of relevant experiences for students or create links with new information (1954).

She emphasizes the centrality of the context and the necessarily interactive nature of the classroom situation. She believes it is the teacher's attitude, value, and skill, conveyed through the relationship with students, rather than technical knowledge and skill, that constitutes the primary element of learning. She alludes to modeling expert behavior as a requisite constituent to the path toward practice mastery. Finally, she emphasizes the need for congruence between the content and skills advanced in the classroom and what happens with students in their practice with actual clients in the field.

David Kolb

Kolb emphasizes the need for discovery and for self-reflection. It is rooted in the idea that education must be grounded in experience and that experience with reflection will result in knowledge acquisition. He joins Dewey and Rogers in emphasizing experience; Towle, Knowles, and Freire in emphasizing involvement; and Schon in emphasizing reflection.

Kolb (1984) describes learning as a four-phase cycle in which the learner: (1) has a concrete or specific experience providing a basis for (2) observation and reflection on the experience and their own response to it. These observations are then (3) assimilated into an abstract conceptualization and are related to other concepts from which implications for action can be derived; and then (4) lead to active experimentation where they are tested and applied in different situations. To learn a new behavior, students must pass through all four stages in order to assimilate information into their personal experience bank. This bank then becomes an additional foundation against which future learning events will be compared and new concepts will be related. Only when what is learned is applied to actual work or life situations is it effective or long-lasting.

Kolb avers that increased self-awareness, changed behavior, and the acquisition of new skills for both you and students results from actively engaging them in the learning process. Kolb's "loop" (1984) suggests that experience is acted upon through reflective observation, which in turn acts as the basis upon which active experimentation followed by feedback produces change. This process encourages in students a strong sense of their own value base and how it relates in turn to professional ethics, theories, and methods. It thereby contributes to developing the ability to make informed choices about what characterizes professional practice.

John Dewey

Dewey (1933), an originator of the concept of reflection as an active and deliberate process, views reflective thinking as "a triumph of reason and science over instinct and impulse." He defines reflective thought as "active, persistent, and careful consideration of any belief or supposed form of knowledge in the light of the grounds that support it and the further conclusion to which it tends" (p. 9). He maintains that reflective learning involves: "(1) a state of doubt, hesitation, perplexity, mental difficulty, in which thinking originates, and (2) an act of searching, hunting, inquiring to find material that will resolve the doubt, settle and dispose of the perplexity" (p. 12).

Dewey views reflective thinking as a means for instilling habits of thought and cultivating self-discipline. It is a worthwhile endeavor because it "converts action that is merely appetitive, blind, and impulsive into intelligent action" (1933, p. 17). It is a way of exercising the imagination toward future possibilities.

Dewey maintains that learning and change are brought about in students though an ongoing cycle of interaction with the environment, an environment in which you, the teacher, play an integral part. Each learning encounter is predicated on previous experiences and affects present and future learning experiences (1933, p. 29).

Dewey continually reiterates that learning best occurs in a social environment. It is by its very character interactive and reciprocal. He criticizes traditional education as a one-way transmission of a codified body of knowledge, differing from a progressive one based in personal experience and experiment. He contends that the quality of experience is key, as is the connection to wider and deeper experiences.

Chiefly, Dewey countered the forced dichotomy and dualism between cognitive and affective learning, the distinction between knowing and doing, experience and knowledge, the individual and the context. He is credited with being a key originator of the concept of reflection and considers it to be a special form of problem-solving (1933). He views it as an active and deliberative cognitive process, one involving sequences of interconnected ideas taking into consideration underlying beliefs and knowledge and allowing for doubt and perplexity before possible solutions are reached.

Dewey also speaks of "reflective action" in which a complete cycle of professional doing needs to be coupled with reflection, ultimately leading to action.

Paulo Freire

In Freire's (1970) thinking, students move toward a fuller and richer life individually and collectively when they are encouraged to act upon and thereby transform their world. He takes a radical departure from the conventional educational paradigm. In his view the educational process needs to become an emancipatory and liberating process of growth. Freire's view is based upon the principle that students are capable of perceiving their personal and social reality, of becoming conscious of their own perception of that reality, and of dealing with it when they have the proper tools. This occurs most especially when interaction with one another is promoted. Engaged in a dialogic exchange, both students and teacher are learners in a mutually constructed learning process. Emerging from this exchange is a new awareness of self, a new sense of dignity, and reinvigorated hope.

In genuine dialogue, the teacher and the learner are intimately engaged with one another. This dialogic encounter replaces the notion of the teacher acting on the student. Dialogue, characterized by cooperation and acceptance of mutuality in the roles of teacher and learner not only deepens understanding, but results in *praxis*, action to make a difference in the world. *Conscientization*—that is, developing critical consciousness—arises from both dialogue and praxis, as well as from situating educational activity directly in the actual lived experience of learners (Freire, 1970).

Freire critiques a banking concept of education. Here the teacher pours information into students. The essence of education rests, rather, on freedom and democracy combined with exploration of generative themes leading to the awakening of critical consciousness. His "pedagogy of hope" prompts us and our students to believe that alternative ways of constructing educational and practice experience are possible.

Freire emphasizes learning as centering on cooperation and acceptance of the interchangeability and mutuality in the roles of teacher and learner. It calls for creating an atmosphere of acceptance and trust, this atmosphere being simultaneously the precursor and the outcome of the educational endeavor. Creation of a responsive and progressive environment for students is vital in a process that is socially and culturally constructed.

Carl Rogers

Rogers advances an instruction theory based on his psychological person-centered orientation. Dealing with the whole person is the central principle in understanding a person from his own perspective rather than from that of the observer. Rogers' concepts endorse the notion that people act as they do because of the ways in which they perceive themselves and the various situations in which they find themselves.

Rogers' view of education faithfully follows his conviction about the importance of affective experiences and total emotional involvement in the learning process. He highlights two types of learning—cognitive learning and experiential learning. Experiential learning is more personally meaningful, as well as more emotionally and cognitively relevant. It has a quality of personal involvement and is relevant because it totally involves the student as a unique person, which is the main path for true learning.

Rogers advances the principle that the instructional method and its objectives are inseparable. His principles of instruction mainly consist of ideas related to creating an emotional and intellectual climate to facilitate experiential learning.

Rogers' educational system can be seen in the outline of the seven practical educational methods he devised to enhance experiential learning. These methods include: (1) focusing on student choice in type of learning situation, traditional structure or free classroom, in which students make their own schedule for learning; (2) use of educational contracts so that students are involved in deciding what should be accomplished; (3) discovery learning, a type of educational structure for acquiring knowledge; (4) simulation, having areas of real-life situations simulated in the classroom by learners so as to experience the situation; (5) sensitivity groups, to help students learn more about themselves; (6) small-group facilitator learning groups, to allow for student participation; and (7) programmed instruction, to allow students to expand their need for information (Rogers, 1983).

Rogers takes the stance of your being a co-learner along with students, someone who recognizes and openly and honestly states your own uncertainties in order to be close to the meaning of experience and fathom the flux of uncertainty.

Overall, Rogers insists on the centrality of the affective dimension of learning. He stresses the need for a climate of safety and proposes the notion that very little learning is achieved on an uninvolved basis and that students do not learn meaningfully, particularly in the professions, if the teacher is too distant or too superior a being.

Donald Schon

Schon (1983) criticizes the technical/rational model as only marginally relevant to the professions. It is based on the idea that "professional activity consists in instrumental problem solving made rigorous by the application of scientific theory and technique" (p. 21).

He expands the ideas of Dewey, Towle, and Rogers and echoes those of Kolb, stressing the role and relevance of experience. But he goes far beyond elaborating upon experience. He believes that involving students as who they are and what they do provides for true education for practice. Stated more forcefully, experience is both the foundation of and stimulus for learning.

Professionals do not learn to practice from the book, especially because they practice in "indeterminate zones," that is, areas involving value conflict and uncertainty. They must rely, therefore, on discretion and improvisation, constantly "inventing and testing in the situation strategies" of their devising (Schon, 1987, p. 5). So, too, the teacher, through processes of modeling, mentoring, and mirroring, prepares the student for such an undertaking.

Schon argues for an approach to teaching that encourages what he aptly refers to as "reflection-in-action." Reflection-in-action is a process-based framework where students come to understand themselves and their actions through the interplay between what they learn to do and what they actually do.

Schon proposes that the reciprocal reflection that occurs between you and students determines the latter's ability to integrate theory into practice, and, furthermore, accounts for their discovering new paradigms for practice. This is one means for distinguishing professional from non-professional practice, since it considers the uncertainty, uniqueness, and conflict inherent in professional practice.

Schon's reflection-in-action is rather spontaneous. It involves making new sense of things, of looping back on experiences in the moment and in novel ways, reconsidering phenomena and the way we approach them. It is not propositional knowledge—descriptions, theories, principles, rules of thumb, but rather knowledge acquired through an interaction with experience that is non-logical, often beyond our control and sudden and unexpected.

Through reflection, the "practitioner allows himself to experience surprise, puzzlement, or confusion in a situation which he finds uncertain or unique. He reflects on the phenomenon before him, and on the prior understandings which have been implicit in his behavior. He carries out an experiment which serves to generate both a new understanding of the phenomenon and a change in the situation" (Schon, 1983, p. 68). This holds true for the teacher as well, who can surface and critique formerly tacit understandings about teaching experiences with a new and unique sense of them. It is accompanied by an increased capacity to exercise judgment in the face of uncertainty.

Schon (1983) contends that reflection-in-action results in the development of a new theory or frame and contributes to the acquisition of professional knowledge after the fact, when action is reconsidered. Reflection-in-action occurs in the moment, during the action. It is a process of being able to be aware of formalities of professional boundaries while being able to work fluidly within them.

Because practice consists of person-to-person interactions, the classroom parallels practice. It is "unavoidably a hall of mirrors in which students read messages" about practice in the teacher/practitioner's behavior—"whether or not he intends to convey them"—and teacher/practitioners read in their students' behavior messages about the students' way of doing professional work. The effectiveness of learning, therefore, depends significantly on the degree to which you "recognize and exploit such mirrorings" so as to make their learning experience a "reflective one in this additional sense" (Schon, 1987, p. 220).

GAPS AND OVERLAPS

In many ways Schon's reflective process reverberates with Dewey's reflective thinking. The aim is to promote a form of professionalism that rejects instrumental and technocratic rationality. A major difference exists, however, in that Schon's discourse on the intuitive contradicts Dewey's association of reflective thinking with the scientific method. Schon, as Kolb, places high value on introspective understanding and non-scientific awareness.

All these perspectives involve the construction of opportunities for learners that systematically support reflection on their previous experience, knowledge, skills, current thinking, and interactions that are activated in the classroom as it transpires. Cues given by the teacher, combined with rigorous reflection, enable students to develop more complex and coherent ideas of practice. Setting the climate for this to occur is critical and largely dependent on the manner in which you create an atmosphere of safety as well as by your own transparency.

A PERSONAL PERSPECTIVE ON REFLECTIVE TEACHING

The ability to contemplate what we do and why we do it is at the heart of professional helping. It involves more than knowing something or performing a task well. It involves internalized dispositions. It involves accessing prior experiences to use in making professional decisions. It is not beholden to reason alone, which may block out other qualities such as values and affects. As academics, we tend to believe that practice and teaching necessarily follows empirical evidence, although we realize that it is not totally true.

Combine in coursework selections from poetry, theater, movies, and literature. These purposefully enhance students' ability to appreciate different perspectives. Fictional situations and characterizations portray actions in penetrating ways, which further enrich students' depth of understanding of humankind. Exposing students to such artistic renditions encourages them to get past any inclination to fit facts to foregone conclusions.

THREE STAGES OF REFLECTION

Reflection is a tripartite endeavor. It includes the ability to consider practice as well as teaching before (pre), during, and after (post) instruction. Reflection has typically been viewed as thinking during or after acting. In addition to these two, consider pre-reflection, before a teaching event. In other words, while much is written in the literature about the second (Kolb, Dewey, Schon) as discussed earlier in this chapter, and both contribute meaningfully to effective teaching, reflection before provides yet another dimension, a great opportunity. These three stages are not hierarchical; each is of equal importance. They are linked. Likewise, they do not necessarily happen in a particular order. Each loops back on and influences the other.

The process is cyclic in that each affects the other. Reviewing a lesson after the fact bears greatly on how the subsequent lesson is conceived. For example, in a course devoted to intensive crisis intervention, students very reluctantly participated in a role play about a threatened suicide attempt. Confounded by such reluctance, I wanted to figure out possible reasons to fathom a way to proceed. Mulling over possible bases for such reticence, a few ideas surfaced. Some of these were fruitful in considering next steps, some seemed extraneous. Nevertheless, pondering a range of options to better conduct the next class was helpful. Among these ideas were: the subject was too charged emotionally; the students were unfamiliar with relevant conceptual material; the students objected to role play as opposed to lecture; students were aware that a classmate had threatened suicide; or too much pressure to role play. Recognizing that it was essential to raise the issue at the subsequent class, two notions were introduced for consideration—that the topic was overly emotionally charged and/or that it was too early in the semester to expect students to engage in role play. Directly discussed, students expressed the belief that both of these factors contributed, allowing us to move on. Forthright discussion set the groundwork for subsequent emotional disclosure and role play.

Reflection encourages you and students to face, observe, and examine performance to better understand what works well and to correct flaws. Your competencies, know-how, and expertise are transferred to students by your active reflection. Your ability to think on your feet, connect with your feelings, and attend to theories as applied instigate close attention to fathoming the whys and wherefores of actions before they transpire, as they unfold, and after they are accomplished. Such a stance captures the essence of professional open-mindedness and tolerance of ambiguity that is expected of students in their work with clients.

Inclusive of theoretical abstraction, technical knowledge, and empirical evidence, reflection involves more than examining textual material, absorbing lectures, participation in role plays, and discussing ideas. It involves knowing what and how you do what you do, but, most important, *why* you do it. It also includes a serious consideration of the impact of what you do. As a corollary, it implicates recognition of what you are not doing and examines why you are not doing it. It necessarily entails explanation and expansion. Reflection at these three junctures resembles, but supercedes, earlier mentioned familiar systems of higher functioning—critical thinking, decision-making, and problem-solving. It ultimately undergirds professional discernment and discretion.

In a nutshell, reflection entails more than abstract theoretical or technical knowledge. It starts with engagement leading to understanding. Understanding enhances performance or action. Reflection on performance leads to higher order thinking, which increases the ability to make sound judgments in the face of constraints and contingencies. It also creates new designs when constraints and unpredictability pertain. These designs result in exercising understanding and applying skills integral to professional identity. Reflection is a form of ownership.

Pre-reflection

There is scant attention to pre-reflection in either the professional or educational literature. It is a vital and integral component in the entire reflection process.

Based on an assessment of your previous lesson, as a tangible outcome of post-reflection, craft your class in advance of your next meeting, employing visualization leading to a lesson plan as described later. Decide on relevant content and work out a plan to present content in the most compelling fashion, using a variety of methods. Consider ways to grab and to hold students' interest. Anticipate how your students will interact from observing them in previous classes. Go beyond instruction; shape the class for maximum engagement.

Five guideline questions regarding this initial pre-reflection phase are: What will I teach? Why should I teach it? How will I teach it? Are there alternatives? What results do I expect and how will they be ascertained?

That you attend so closely to reviewing and reconsidering lessons in this stage does not imply that you rigidly adhere to that plan. To do so would violate the very idea of ongoing scrutiny and concomitant flexibility.

During Reflection

Schon considers this component of the reflective process to be the most difficult to achieve. He calls it "reflection-in-action." It is characterized by what I refer to as the split screen, that is, conducting an action experiment on the spot, as described earlier. What makes it so difficult is that it is simultaneously calculative and contemplative. One way of describing this stage is that you are at the same time the performer and the critic.

Reflection is often thought of as a solitary and meditative task. It does not need to be. It can be achieved in isolation but is enriched—indeed, superior— when publicly and collaboratively undertaken. When immediate feedback is elicited, step back and ask, "What am I doing?" "Why am I doing it?" "With what result?"

Dialogue is an essential ingredient. Your ability to navigate between the conceptual and experiential ushers in for students the necessity to integrate the two domains. Your responsibility as a teacher is to raise, organize, and summarize what is going on to reinforce the connection between experience and cognitive understanding.

Remain open, self-critical, flexible, spontaneous, and creative. Tolerate ambiguity. Run a commentary upon theory being employed in class and your own take on proceedings. Expose your personal lens on your approach; it invites students to identify their own.

Reflection by nature is inductive, having its origin in experience, rather than deductive, beginning with concepts and theories. Your challenge is to marry both so that students witness how to bridge the artificial gulf between ideas and intuitions, science and art.

Some alternative pre-reflection questions to assist your reflection-in-action during teaching are: What am I teaching? Why am I teaching it? How am I teaching it? How are students responding? Are there alternatives? What are the results?

Questions such as these stimulate students in discovering the basic tools of professional inquiry.

Post-reflection

Resembling Schon's reflection-on-action, post-reflection epitomizes the adage, "hindsight is 20/20." In other words, post-reflection is not simply recollection but reclaims experience and invents new approaches and reinforces other ones that prove practical and pertinent. These second thoughts provide a keen and introspective look backward before going forward. Post-reflection can be achieved through close monitoring of your lesson after the fact in a variety of ways—listening to audiotapes and viewing videotapes of the lesson, referring to notes taken as the lesson was delivered, evaluatory comments from students given during and at the end of a class, and journaling. The relevance and usefulness of keeping a teaching journal is addressed later in this book. It systematically evokes and strengthens your command of the teaching process. In any event, be sure to take time to ponder your lesson after the fact; take stock of both the big picture as well as the discrete elements. Being candid with yourself will enable you to figure out the reasons for your lesson's success or the reasons why it may have faltered. Such data offers you the opportunity to accentuate and replicate its execution or take corrective action in the future.

Ask yourself, "What is going on with me?" "What is going on with my students?" Search for the underlying ideas that constitute your own system of understanding and delivery. Take risks, do not stick simply with the familiar. Open up new ventures and diversify formats and modalities.

Mapping the lesson is a strategy I utilize in a doctoral course spotlighting the principle, processes, and practices of professional education. At the end of each class, particularly because its focal point is teaching, time is taken to systematically reconstruct, review, and reconsider the dynamic ebb and flow of the lesson. Were the quotations apt? Were the cartoons instructive? Were the required readings useful? Did the body of the lesson cohere? Was there sufficient variety in method? What other methods might have proved more effective? Overall, what other ways could content be transmitted? How might it be delivered differently? This debriefing interprets and illuminates the lesson's notable productive or ineffective features, addresses questions or issues not yet examined, and assesses the lesson's global effect.

As in the pre and during stages of reflection, the following questions, closely paralleling the others, may help you focus attention on the variables of your lesson: What did I teach? Why did I teach it? How did I teach it? Were there alternatives? How did students respond? What were the results? What next?

The interplay of pre-, during, and post-reflection may be seen in table 3.

BALANCING SEEMING CONTRADICTIONS

Your credibility as a reflective teacher depends upon your ability to balance seemingly contradictory qualities simultaneously—holding onto your values and views while entertaining contrasting, even contradictory, ones;

Table 3. Phases of Lesson Plan Reflection

Pre	During	Post
What will I teach?	What am I teaching?	What did I teach?
Why should I teach it?	Why am I teaching it?	Why did I teach it?
How will I teach it?	How am I teaching it?	How did I teach it?
Are there alternatives?	Are there alternatives?	Were there alternatives?
What results do I expect and how will they be ascertained?	What are the results?	What were the results?
	How are students responding?	How did students respond?
		What next?

being critical of self while being confident; being honest and public with insights while earnestly and privately sharpening them. It calls for examining your impact, exploring alternatives, listening to student feedback either tacitly or explicitly given, elicited or spontaneous, verbal or nonverbal. It demands self-scrutiny, discussed later in this chapter, to ascertain if you are doing the very thing that you ask students to do in a conscious, deliberate, and purposeful manner.

The aim of reflection is to integrate understanding gained with upcoming experience in order to make better decisions about what to present as well as to enhance overall understanding and performance effectiveness.

In summary, reflection is both cognitive and affective; requires active engagement; is sparked by an unusual or perplexing situation or experience; demands examining responses, beliefs, and premises in light of the situation at hand; and results in integration of new understanding into the students' experiences. New understanding resulting from reflection leads to broadened and deepened learning, an enhanced array of choices, and a more sophisticated capacity to choose among these choices and implement them effectively.

Methods such as journaling, modeling, critical incidents, movies, tapes, and so on, elucidated in later chapters, help you and, in the long run, your students to develop skills in reflection and enhance the teaching/learning process. Deliberate and planned reflection of the kind articulated here is dependent to a great degree on your awareness of your self. Self-awareness leads to, and results from, reflection.

SELF-AWARENESS

It is axiomatic that self-awareness is a prerequisite for undertaking effective professional activity. Although historically articulated in different ways, the concept of growing in self-understanding has been acknowledged as an essential component in all forms of practice (individual, family, group, community, as well as teaching) and at every level of engagement (clinical, supervisory, and educational). Practice as well as teaching involves concern for the objective other as well as concern for the subjective self.

Rogers puts it this way: "Can I hear the sounds and sense the shape of this other person's inner world? Can I resonate to what he is saying so deeply that I sense the meanings he is afraid of yet would like to communicate, as well as those he knows?" (1980, p. 8). Reflection, coming to grips with self, rather than trying to explain ourselves according to theories, produces heightened understanding of ourselves in relation to current clients and students, and ultimately to every new client and student.

A prerequisite for effectiveness is a keen sense of one's inwardness of self. The benchmark is a sense of mindfulness. There is insufficient attention paid in the professional and educational literature to fostering self-awareness.

Your constant challenge is understanding the interplay between your personal and professional roles and responses. This is an especially difficult endeavor. It denotes by its very nature an interrelationship between your inner world and the outer world of your work. Practitioners and teachers alike are expected to rely upon their knowledge, expertise, experience, and training to fathom their subjectivity both for its own sake and so as not to interpose one's predispositions on others. By accessing your self, you show to students an example of how to confront their own selves. What guides you in doing so is engaging in a systematic inventory of your personal beliefs, traits, and characteristic behaviors. Accessing your self means being willing to be vulnerable and open to experiencing previously unknown aspects of yourself.

It has been emphasized that only when you are alert to who you are and what you are doing are you sufficiently relaxed, clear, and open-minded to understand others.

Your personality, values, and sensitivity are the very tools that make you an effective educational instrument. They influence what happens in your interaction with students. Your *personhood*, in other words, is the essential feature in the establishment and maintenance of a teacher-and-student alliance. This alliance has been portrayed using other terms, all basically alluding to the same phenomenon: for example, partnership and mutuality.

Draw upon your own self in the service of students as a guide to their increased self, client, theoretical, and empirical understanding. Since you can react only from what is within you, you must know yourself so that your capacity for being in relationship is increased, your ability to react consciously is intensified, and you are freer to make deliberate choices about how to respond to students. Only by knowing yourself are you in a position to make active and creative use of your knowledge, skills, values, and intentions for them.

Examine your beliefs and biases. Find compatibility between them and your feelings and behavior. Scrutinize your basic assumptions. Search out what you truly cherish. Such awareness leads to more disciplined and clearly directed teaching practice. As a personal example, I recognize that my predilection for highlighting the unconscious aspects of behavior emanates from an earlier background in psychodynamic theory. If unchecked, it imposes a particular slant on interaction with students and interpretation of case material.

When you make mistakes in class in matters of theory or misinterpreting student queries or responses, as you are bound to do because you are human, accept and acknowledge them openly and directly. Recognize, too, that mistakes are not necessarily irreparable; on the contrary, they may be valuable. They constitute grist for the learning mill. They may provide unexpected and unplanned-for lessons about the efficacy of making assessments and interventions. Acknowledging mistakes allows you to participate more fully in the teaching relationship. Furthermore, it enables students to accept their own mistakes.

In brief, do what you expect students to do. Take a hard and close look at your *self*.

Assume responsibility for your actions and reactions.

Think hard about your role. How might you act differently? What innovative methods do you try? What do you bring to teaching in terms of special talents and insights? Visualize specific ways in which you present yourself and how you behave both in times of stability and crisis.

Share yourself and your methods openly yet selectively. When you are accessible and open about your practice and teaching triumphs and struggles, students will not only see you as more human, but as someone who can understand how they feel, as someone who faces obstacles much like their own yet manages to learn and succeed. What will be most helpful to them is seeing not only someone who knows what he is talking about but knows what they are talking about.

SELF-AWARENESS IN A HISTORICAL PERSPECTIVE

Historically, self-awareness has been defined in differing ways—personality, recognition of self and of difference, or awareness of and responsibility for one's feelings and attitudes. Self-awareness is deemed as insight into how your personality, knowledge, and expertise affects you and your interaction with others.

In her seminal work, *The Learner in Education for the Professions*, Towle (1954) considers the conscious and the unconscious factors inherent in the education of a practitioner. She speaks of the need to become "receptive to insight and thus come to think objectively in situations . . . and to understand his feelings, emotions, and attitudes as they affect . . . work" (1954, p. 164). She amplifies on this theme by stating that the "responsible professional worker cannot permit himself the comfort of becoming deeply unconscious of self. He must always be consciously attentive to the import of his activity" (1954, p. 37).

The most helpful attitudes and behaviors of the professional were described by Rogers (1958) as being authentic and honest, personally identifying with others' issues, and using self-disclosure. Of considerable moment is attending to the impact of self.

Dewey alludes to self-awareness. Underlying his philosophy of education is recognition of the imprint of the subjective experience (what he would term "experience and nature"). He suggests that inner awareness encompasses a vital constituent of the process of inquiry.

Schon (1983, 1987) implies that teachers need first to search for the underlying ideas that constitute their system of understanding and then to communicate that to students to assist them in developing their own.

Kolb (1984) avers that increased self-awareness is a key ingredient pursuant to changed behavior. The acquisition of new skills results from actively engaging students in the learning process and highlighting self-reflection.

The clear consensus obviously among these writers is that self-realization is of paramount importance. Introspection does not displace content and substance but enhances it with an architecture that includes experience, intuition, awareness, and integration.

Frequently cited is the caution that it is only when you know who you are that you can be sufficiently clear and open-minded about what you are doing. It is impossible to be tuned into the work at hand without first being attuned to one's self. Self-awareness is a precondition for competent, culturally sensitive practice across the professional spectrum of activity.

Although it is often considered otherwise, teachers are not totally detached from their occupational tasks. As human beings, both practitioners and teachers have aspirations, fears, and commitments that influence how they think and how they go about formulating questions and methodologies to examine issues, problems, and dilemmas. Typical teachers are not fully objective, free-thinking, and skeptical. They are conservative by nature in the way they apply knowledge.

Self-awareness requires conscious choice. In this regard, it is not viewed as an attained state but rather as an ongoing value. It is in flux, not an end product. Take the process seriously and devote time and effort to explore it. How you achieve self-awareness or, rather, how you continually expand your self-understanding constitutes a progression involving cognitive, emotional, and social elements.

PART II
Effective Processes

Humans do not enter the world with minds, but with brains. The task of education . . . is to convert brains into minds. Brains are born. Minds are made; and one of the privileges of the teaching professions is to have an important part to play in the shaping of minds.

—ELLIOT EISNER

HELPING STUDENTS establish a sound and solid professional identity and preparing them for effective professional functioning results from your taking stock of their alacrity, rousing their curiosity, maintaining their enthusiasm, educing their intellect and affect. Your careful attention to involving them in shaping course content and direction, to their style of learning and your own style of teaching, and to charting stimulating lessons contributes to an environment conducive to shaping professional minds.

The following two chapters—learning and teaching styles and lesson planning, emerge naturally from earlier ones. They concentrate on ways to draw upon relationship and reflection to translate the theoretical, philosophical, and abstract ideas into deliverable lessons.

Advance preparation is advocated principally through giving ample attention to developing a lesson plan, the vehicle for organizing your content, format, and presentation methods. Lesson plans maximize learning and better assure your meeting course expectations. Students are seekers. Treat their experience and ideas as pivotal. Invite students to share their goals and expectations. Discuss how these mesh with your own and what can be done to accommodate them. Articulate your own biases, beliefs, stances, and pet peeves. Explain how you've implemented changes to your approach based on former students' comments and recommendations.

Taking students past rote learning toward heightened understanding, integration, and, ultimately, application in new circumstances takes diligent attention to encouraging conceptualization and differentiation in both the cognitive and emotional spheres. You play a direct role in developing these spheres by designing lessons that appeal to students' varying learning styles. Since students have differences in the way knowledge is assimilated, conceptualized, valued, judged, and reacted to, your attending to these increases your ability to adjust your own style so as best to appeal to students' strengths and, in so doing, motivate them and facilitate success in learning.

Intersecting Styles: Teaching to Strengths

To be a teacher in the right sense is to be a learner. Instruction begins when you, the teacher, learn from the learner, put yourself in his place so that you may understand what he understands and the way he understands it.

—SØREN KIERKEGAARD

While there may be "born teachers" with superb potential, no one is born a teacher ready simply to walk into a classroom and shine. They are born as persons who become teachers shaped by life, which influences the style they bring to the classroom to empower students. It makes sense as well to ensure that students learn in ways that are relevant to their preferred learning styles. It ensures learning that is meaningful, exciting, and challenging.

No two people learn in the same way. No two people teach or practice the same way. Research on personality, left/right brain functioning, and on learning suggest that learning and teaching is a uniquely personal process. Each of you has a different speed, rhythm, and attention span. While we possess a variety of common characteristics as learners and as teachers, you also have discrete differences. These individual patterns are referred to as styles. Style is a pattern of preferences displayed for associating information with other stored experiences. Each of you as well as each of your students has a uniquely personal style. Style refers to *how* learning occurs, rather than *how well* it occurs. How do these styles intersect? Can they be matched? We know that when an alien speed, rhythm, or attention span is imposed on us, little or no learning occurs. Resistance and fatigue result.

Teaching style consists of your personal conduct and preferences for the content and the way you transmit it. It depends as well on your conception of education. People learn in different ways, and your own style makes demands on learners and influences your use of materials and structure. Stretching

57

your style and using different methods, observing and discussing students' styles, and becoming acquainted with techniques that appeal to both right and left brain functions intensify learning. Aligning these factors places considerable demands on you.

Teachers well-versed in their disciplines are naturally concerned about covering the topics in syllabi. Too often, however, they over-rely on packaged lectures to do so. Brain research suggests that it is important to shake out of such routinization. Doing so keeps you fresh and alert and makes your lessons vibrant. It provides students with novel takes on content and time to process and integrate new information.

Many contextual factors go into determining the way you learn and teach best. These include: preferred environment, emotional climate, social and physical setting, structure, cultural factors, sensory modalities, reasoning patterns, and memory influences. Learning depends as well upon an awareness of the centrality of relationships, your style, and the styles of students.

Expand your own style to galvanize strengths or compensate for limitations through the use of specific strategies, materials, and experimentation with alternative techniques. Make adaptations to maximize learning. Engaging in such a process crystallizes your relationship with students and advances reflection.

Questions guiding a consideration of style are: What is my style? How does it affect classes? Is it an exclusive style? What do I like and dislike about it? Do I need to modify my style? What effects, both negative and positive, would any change have on my teaching effectiveness? What do I need to do in order to modify my style? Do I prefer to learn/teach by discussion or guest speakers; diagrams, charts, or slides; field trips, labs, or practice sessions; handouts or textbooks? The self-refection and assessment that these questions stimulate lead to choices among alternative possibilities for more fully ensuring engagement with students. Questions about student patterns parallel ones about your own: What are their styles? How are they manifested? What methods arouse their attention? Which keep them focused? Which generate excitement?

CHARACTERISTICS OF STYLES

People differ in the way they perceive, receive, and convey information and experiences; in the way they process and think about what they take in and let out; in the way they react to and value what they think about; and how they behave in the learning situation.

Some prefer to receive information visually, while others learn best by hearing new ideas and discussing concepts. Some need the global idea, the big picture, while others learn best by taking one small step at a time. Some dive right in and want an immediate hands-on experience, while others lay back and want to slowly absorb theory and concepts.

Some think linearly and sequentially, while others jump around and connect in various ways with other experiences. Some favor logic and rationality, while others gravitate toward the emotional and intuitive.

Reactions to new information also vary. Some students react in an overt way, nod their heads, raise their hands, and ask questions while others are more internal. Some are more concerned with process (how), while others focus on content (what). Some immediately judge new information by its effect on others; others are concerned with the evidence that it will work. Some students like to work alone; others respond best in groups.

As mentioned earlier in the chapter, your style of teaching is influenced largely by your conception or philosophy of professional education. Do you see yourself as someone who guides and directs students toward their own learning? Someone who shares your own wisdom and experience? Attempts to change students' views of the world? Helps students to apply theory in a practical way? Develops critical thinking or curiosity? Imparts information? Challenges students to understand phenomena deeply? Encourages students to question existing modes of thinking? Invites discourse and controversy? Bolsters skills? Develops self-awareness?

Your outlook has great bearing on your style and approach.

STYLES AS WINDOWS ON THE WORLD

We see the world though the windows of our personalities and styles. Even though each window view is unique and different from every other, each window also shares certain similarities. When the windows are grouped by similarities, patterns emerge.

Real windows have frames, and the frames direct attention to a certain part of the scenery, emphasizing one part, minimizing another. Real windows also sometimes have screens, which can distort the views. The windows of our minds also have frames and screens, which affect what we see as well as how we respond to what we see. We perceive certain elements and not others because our experience is filtered through the screens of cognitive processes, preferences, values, experiences, and so on.

The windows and screens we use determine, either as students or as teachers, how we process information about the world—how we take in what is happening, how we give meaning to it, how we send out information to others. Recognizing and acknowledging these different windows can maximize effectiveness.

Beyond your obligation to look past your preferred panes, as it were, your obligation is to scrutinize what is beyond. Who sits in front of you? How do they attend to what occurs in the room? Ponder the array of students' learning styles to insure the most effective learning venture. Understanding learning styles allows you to tailor the content of the lesson to students' characteristics and class composition, thereby promoting more open and active participation.

Students operate on different levels and will not all catch on at the same time. Find ways to give different students different kinds of challenges. With pre-reflection you can accommodate a variety of styles within a single lesson.

When you plan a lesson, take style into special consideration. Stay in sync with students' preferred styles. Different students will integrate similar material when offered in different forms. Use various methods of instruction, vary assignments, and offer options for learners whenever possible. Talk with students about their preferences, seek feedback on your style, and solicit ideas for strategies.

Keep in mind that you, like students, have preferred techniques of exposition, fashioning courses, and relating to others. Among these modes are lecture, role play, and discussion, many of which are addressed in subsequent chapters. None of these are either better or worse than any other; rather, each has advantages and each has drawbacks. Attempt to achieve balance in the way you assemble your lesson. Try to be flexible in your approach. Modify your characteristic style. Different results are best achieved with different methods with different students. For example, abstract conceptualizers respond well to lecture and discussion. Attitudinal and affective learners relate to such experiential methods as role play and case presentation. If you rely solely upon one or two familiar, tried-and-true forms of delivery, realize that they may not appeal to certain students, and the lesson may falter because of it. Endeavor instead to match the specific content and method of instruction to the context.

Take the opportunity to reflect on how you might stretch your style. Experiment with varying modes of delivery to assess what best suits you, the content, and the students. This may change from lesson to lesson and course to course. Your approach may require continual retooling and fine-tuning. Consider what does not work. Recognize and build on what does work. Seek to discover and test out alternative channels.

THE FIRST TWO PANES: COGNITION AND CONCEPTUALIZATION

Perception, the initial stage of cognition, involves receiving and discerning information, ideas, and concepts. There are many different ways of perceiving. Some students separate out parts from wholes; some attend to what is in the foreground, some to the background. Given a choice, students will generally respond consistently more one way than another. Their perceptual styles affect *what* they receive and *how* they receive it, what is learned and how learning takes place. Learning is optimized when you accommodate to students' perceptual strengths. Likewise, naturally, to accommodate to students' preferences, you need first to be aware of your own favored pattern of cognition and conceptualization, as the following example illustrates:

> Mr. R, a mature student interning in a community center, expressed concern in a class on interviewing that he felt he was missing parts of his interview with "Marge," a depressed woman there. He didn't know why. It wasn't, he felt, for lack of practice—his previous job, in fact, had involved interviewing people at a public benefits center to determine their eligibility for income maintenance.
>
> His interviewing technique, however, hewed closely to the mandated protocol of his former job, where he was discouraged from employing discretion, eliciting feelings, or assessing motivation. He did not delve into clients' attitudes and affects. His was a prescribed form of interviewing—almost an interrogation. Partly as a result, Mr. R felt uncomfortable with both the flexible and affective dimension of a more clinical interview. Familiar with Mr. R's style from previous classes, his clinical practice teacher opened discussion, eventuating in a role play in which Mr. R, playing the practitioner, recognized, as did the entire class observing the role play, how his rigid manner and unrealistic demands have a negative impact on clients.

Following is another instance of differing perceptual styles:

> Mr. Z and Ms. L, two students viewing a videotape of a family session by an eminent therapist during a class in family-oriented treatment, responded quite differently to Dr. B's interventions depicted on the screen. Mr. Z, coming from a corporate background, noticed immediately the explicit and direct verbal messages of Dr. B and their subsequent impact on the W family. Ms. L, on the other hand, spotted the effect of Dr. B's indirect nonverbal cues on the family and its subtle response to them. Dr. F, their professor, capitalized on their distinct but complementary manner of viewing the interventions by encouraging them to explain their different views. Each enriched the other's acuity and fostered in both a more total and penetrating picture that provided the class observing their dialogue with a more comprehensive depiction of the interplay and sway of verbal and nonverbal interaction.

Students gain knowledge in different ways. Teachers dispense knowledge in different ways. Some use abstract sources, others need concrete examples. Ponder some parallels to teaching. The "concrete" student often depends upon his or her senses for knowledge: "I see it, therefore I know what it is." The "abstract" student, on the other hand, is more receptive to second-hand sources of knowledge. There are even sensory specialists—those who rely on one sense almost exclusively to gather information. Some students rely on internal sources, some on external, and some use both. Again, these different ways students get information and gain knowledge reflect distinct learning styles. There are students who have to touch something or see it operate before they accept its value, and others who operate in another way, thus:

> Mr. D, another mature student placed in a local senior service center, who learned by doing, was encouraged in his practice class to dive into organizing a group of members to advocate for a lunch program. Mr. D reported back to class the details and successful outcome of this endeavor. His colleague, Ms. G, on the other hand, before undertaking a similar task was encouraged first to read selected articles provided by the professor in order to conceptualize the process before actually attempting to act on it. Dr. O, their teacher/practitioner maximized the effectiveness of each student because he appreciated and fostered their individual learning styles.

Students also exhibit differences in what they do with the knowledge they gain—how they process information. Some students look for connections, for ways of tying things together. Others take a more divergent slant. Some teachers take seemingly irrelevant detours without getting back to the main point. One thought, idea, or fact triggers a multitude of new associations and directions. Students and teachers also show inductive or deductive reasoning preferences.

> Challenging a student in a clinical seminar, for example, Dr. M queried, "What made you arrive at a diagnosis of 'narcissistic personality disorder' for Mr. C?" He then realized that the student, "Laura," looking at the client's seemingly self-aggrandizing self-presentation from a popular rather than a professional context, was thinking about Mr. C without the benefit of having studied *DSM* criteria. Dr. M took the occasion to briefly lecture the class on this manual and the difference between *narcissistic* and *borderline* personality disorder, borderline being the diagnosis Dr. M ascribed to Mr. C.

It is essential for you to realize and be open to the fact that your students perceive, gain knowledge, and process knowledge in different ways. These differences are stylistic and affect your teaching as well as their learning behavior. Draw upon them differently and utilize them flexibly to enhance the learning experience.

THE THIRD PANE: AFFECT

Differences in motivation, ways of making judgments, and responding emotionally to tasks also characterize individual styles. Some students seek to please, others seem oblivious to your reactions. Some object to demands and requirements. Some seek continual feedback about their work and are crushed by the slightest criticism; others won't feel they've done a good job without some constructive criticism. Some students never ask teachers for their opinions. Others never cease doing so. Some have strong preferences for particular experiential techniques, while others focus exclusively on the content didactically delivered in lecture form. Some prefer being spoon fed and others prefer being given a fork. Some concentrate fully on a lecture, ignoring distractions, and are persistent in staying with a task until it is finished. Others stray, glaze over, and tune out in response to verbiage. Some students respond expressively, others remain neutral, and others are stone-faced. The expressive student, for example, prefers a classroom situation with a high emotional charge, while others work best in a low-key environment.

These affective differences are interrelated with the conceptual and cognitive characteristics and influence how students absorb, process, and integrate knowledge and skill. They also shape the teacher/practitioner's modus operandi.

THE FOURTH PANE: BEHAVIOR

Behavior points to how students apply learning. Some are thoughtful and others are impulsive. Reflective students are slow to respond, carefully formulating a response before they act. Impulsive students value a quick response. There are differences in sequential patterns as well. The step-by-step student learns when each step is clear and the transitions are spelled out, moving incrementally from one tread to the next. Another typically takes intuitive leaps. For example, after several weeks of struggling with the concept of projective identification, Ms. A suddenly cried, "I've got it!" identifying and accurately interpreting the complex idea. Ms. Y, on the other hand, slowly gained understanding of the concept after hearing it pointed out repeatedly in diverse ways accompanied by an array of explanations and examples. Progress in each of these situations is made because Ms. A's and Ms. Y's senses of achievement are brought about through carefully selected learning opportunities and support for reaching their individual plateaus.

There are also differences in problem-solving approaches. Some students scan a situation to get the gist before tackling a problem, while others focus on a specific item immediately. Some approach problems randomly, others are very systematic. Some students need explicit structure, while others prefer and perform best in an open-ended structure. Some students prefer to work alone, others with groups, and some prefer working in certain physical environments and conditions over others.

THE CLASSROOM REALITY

Teaching style governs the reality of the classroom. No two teachers will use an exercise, a case record, or a text in exactly the same way. Each one of you personally attempts to make the curriculum come alive for students as well as yourselves. Your style and your recognition of that of your students is manifested by your professional behavior in the way you relate to students, in how you structure and manage your classroom, the mood and tone you set in your classrooms, and the methods and materials you select to help students learn. It is manifested as well by the curriculum you have chosen to emphasize, and by your priorities and strategies for evaluation.

Your knowledge of learning styles allows the revision and adaptation of your own style in order to appeal to students' style strengths, recognize and appreciate their differences, and develop assorted strategies to facilitate success.

To match teaching style with learning style seems to make obvious sense. That it were so simple! When you afford students the opportunity to express themselves through their particular styles, they will feel honored in the classroom and good about the learning they accomplish. Your goal is not to teach specifically to certain learning styles only. Nor is the goal to remove difficult opportunities from the students' experiences. The goal is to initiate and sustain a process of surveying students' learning styles, recognizing your own, and finding correspondence between them.

Although most students learn primarily through one style, they likely have characteristics of other styles. This is also true for you.

Style from Two *Almost* Complementary Perspectives

A number of conceptions and definitions of learning style have been proposed, each possessing some degree of plausibility. Howard Gardner's book, *Frames of Mind: The Theory of Multiple Intelligences* (1983), popularized the idea of uniqueness in the ways in which we perceive and grasp phenomena. He identified relatively independent forms of processing information including verbal, logical, visual, bodily, musical, interpersonal, and intrapersonal. In *Five Minds for the Future* (2007), he made facile and easy to absorb his comparison of "lumpers" and "splitters." "Lumpers" see connections, join ideas together, accentuate commonalities. "Splitters" make distinctions, see differences and contrasts. While there is widespread agreement about the existence of individual differences in styles, there is great difference in the ways researchers and theoreticians examine and conceptualize them. Some describe cognitive processes; some describe personality characteristics, some behaviors. As a consequence, there is disagreement about the validity of these theories. No one approach is either conclusive or all-encompassing. Each separate one, when woven into a whole fabric, contributes to better understanding the nature and relevance of individual learning styles. There is variance in the way teachers teach. Regardless of their empirical validity, learning style theories have heuristic value in calling attention to the fact that people differ and that it is of paramount importance to account for these differences in ourselves, our students, and, ultimately, our clients.

Gardner (1983) made an important contribution to the literature about learning styles by proposing the notion of multiple intelligences. The psychological and educational perspectives from Jung and Kolb respectively, however, offer more specific, comprehensive, and pragmatic outlooks. They complement each other. As mentioned earlier, neither is strictly reliable and valid on empirical terms, neither has a corner on the concept, but, especially taken together, they offer noteworthy food for thought.

Carl Jung (seen mostly from Myers and Briggs)

Jung (1971) and some of the work emerging from his seminal contributions, principally Myers and Briggs, described four primary learning and personality functions—the ability to (1) think clearly and logically; (2) feel and respond emotionally to people and experiences; (3) respond to the immediate and act as necessary; and finally, the ability to (4) imagine, speculate, and envision. While all human beings are capable of all four basic functions, Jung believed that people developed mental preferences.

The first set of mental preferences refers to how information is perceived, or taken in. There are those teachers and students who prefer sensing (clear, tangible data and information that fits with direct, here-and-now experience), and in contrast, there are those who prefer intuiting (information that is more abstract, conceptual, and represents imaginative possibilities for the future). The second set of mental preferences identifies how people form judgments or make decisions after having perceived. Those who prefer thinking have a natural preference for making decisions in an objective, logical, and analytical manner with an emphasis on tasks and results to be accomplished. Those whose preference is for feeling, however, make their decisions in a rather global, visceral, and value-oriented way, paying particular attention to the impact of decisions on other people. These four primary types, which would characterize learners and teachers, are aptly labeled *sensors, intuitors, thinkers*, and *feelers*.

Jung's theory of types provides one model enabling us to understand why people differ in the ways they take in information (perception) and make decisions (judgment). Although not spelled out with any detail in this chapter, an additional function that contributes to overall style is what Jung referred to as orientation—being introverted or extroverted. Introversion relates to the process of responding to stimulation arising from within, from the inner world of thoughts and reflections. Extroversion, on the other hand, relates to the process of responding to stimulation arising from the outer world of people and things.

Katharine Cook Briggs and her daughter, Isabel Briggs Myers (1976), studied Jung's work and expanded Jung's definitions of types to a model that identifies sixteen specific types of individuals. They developed the Myers-Briggs Type Indicator. It measures two alternate modes of perception: sensing or intuiting; two kinds of judgment: feeling or thinking; two sources of primary-interest focus; extravert or introvert; and two types of preference; judging or perceiving. They differentiate sixteen distinct types of people with different styles of perception, judgment, relationships, and personality. These types absorb, respond, and learn differently. And they affect the manner in which teacher/practitioners teach. Again, the four most straightforward types as they pertain to teaching are sensor, intuitor, thinker, and feeler.

Sensors   look for what is immediate and real. They focus on the here and now and readily translate ideas into action. They work steadily and consistently, following through until reaching a conclusion. Patient with routine and precise with details and action-oriented, they accomplish tasks in a down-to-earth, energetic manner. Pragmatically inclined, concrete, and relentless in pursuit of results, they make things happen. Sensor students and teacher/practitioners resemble each other in being partial to handouts, identifying next steps, and reliance on literal and specific details.

Intuitors   grasp possibility and are imaginative. They respond insightfully to abstraction and make dramatic leaps of ideas, often jumping to conclusions. Invested in the world of possibilities, they value innovation and long-range thinking. Probing as their hallmark, they have an uncanny ability to anticipate and to project. Sometimes thought of as visionaries, they typically work in bursts of energy powered by enthusiasm and see connections between things that others do not comprehend. They follow their inspirations. Teachers in this domain play with metaphors, big ideas, leaps of association. Students in this sphere easily follow along.

Thinkers   seek order and plan according to impersonal logic and tend to assess situations by organizing and analyzing information in a rational fashion. They prefer to make decisions unemotionally and are disinterested in others' feelings. Analysis and systematic inquiry are their hallmark. Cool, steady, and skeptical, they find satisfaction in identifying an issue, developing a variety of possible solutions, weighing them carefully, and testing them out. This applies to both students and teachers.

Feelers   try to find harmony in situations, valuing subjective values and personal emotional manner. They have high concern for people, tend to be aware of and sympathetic toward others' circumstances and positions. Able to read between the lines, sensitive, and warm, they gravitate toward dynamic and stimulating experiences involving people. They are perceptive and insightful and have the capacity to sort out complex situations, interpret meanings, and assess the climate or morale of a group. Student feelers tend to like group experiences, emotionally laden case material, and sharing personal experiences. Teacher/practitioner feelers gravitate to experiential methods such as role play and exploratory exercises.

Each of us uses a blend of all four processes, but for each type one of the four processes assumes a dominant role, and it becomes the guide post for learning and teaching. Other processes operate but are subordinate to and serve the dominant function.

As with Kolb, whose theory follows, Jung believed that there is a mutual usefulness in the opposites, a yin for every yang. In other words, intuitive types need sensors to bring up pertinent facts and remember things that were not relevant at the time they happened in order to keep track of details. Sensors need intuitives to see possibilities, to supply ingenuity, to deal with complex issues having many imponderables, to explain what another intuitive is talking about, to look ahead and furnish new ideas, to add spark to things that seem impossible. Thinkers need feelers to persuade and conciliate, to arouse enthusiasm, to appreciate, to give warm acceptance and feedback. Feelers need thinkers to analyze, to organize, to weigh evidence, to be consistent, and to hold firm against opposition.

David Kolb

Kolb (1984) defines learning as "the process whereby knowledge is created through the transformation of experience" (p. 18). Two essential concepts prevail: how learners assimilate new information and how they process and integrate it. He suggests that learning has two distinct dimensions. The first he calls "prehension," or grasping, echoing Jung's "perceiving" function. The second dimension he calls "transforming," or processing, corresponding to Jung's "judging" function. Prehension has two subdivisions characterized as concrete experiences and abstract conceptualizations. Transforming also has two subdivisions, reflective observation and active experimentation.

In his four-stage model, Kolb proposes that learning requires opposite abilities (recall Jung) and that the learner has to continually choose which set of learning abilities to bring to bear in any specific situation. He sees successful learning as a constant tension between action and observation, involvement and reflection. He proposes that students have a unique way of learning, have strengths and weaknesses, and, as a result of hereditary equipment, life experience, and the demands of the environment, most develop styles that emphasize some learning abilities over others.

In identifying the two dimensions of how people learn, Kolb believes that individuals intercept information somewhere along a continuum. Those at the concrete end of the continuum sense and feel their way into material. They enter into the experience. Others tend to be abstract; they think their way into the material. They stand outside the experience and examine it. Some students process by reflecting and watching, others jump right in and try it. These process by doing. When these two dimensions are juxtaposed, four learning styles emerge.

Kolb (1984) posits that learning occurs as students progress through a four-step cycle of concrete experiences, reflective observations, abstract conceptualizations, and, finally, active experimentations. This cycle is successive and becomes increasingly complicated as students devise generalizations that enable them to combine various observations into explanations. These generalizations serve as maps that allow students to explore and participate in experimenting. When students tour the cycle, then repeat it, they become more receptive to various learning types, become increasingly challenged, as well as acquire increased ability to learn how to learn.

Kolb distinguishes four learning styles—*divergers*, *assimilators*, *convergers*, and *accommodators*.

Divergers   perceive concretely with their senses and feelings, and process effectively by watching. They are reflective sensor-feelers. Having a receptive, experience-based approach, they rely heavily on feeling-based judgments and are identified as being creative. They are able to examine events and situations from various viewpoints and bring together that information into a meaningful whole. They are adept at collecting ideas and conceptualizing.

Assimilators   depend on their intellect and process reflectively by watching. They are reflective thinkers who are impartial and prefer to watch and ponder what is going on and understand by careful observation. Able to see several different points of view, they generate many ideas about how things happen, and are strong in developing theoretical paradigms. Attracted to abstract concepts, more interested in theories than in how they are operationalized, they assimilate and synthesize information into consolidated wholes.

Convergers   perceive with their intellect and process actively. They are doing-thinkers. Analytical and conceptual in their approach, they rely on logical thinking and evaluation. They respond to the opportunity to integrate new learning with what is already known and from theory. Preferring to think things through, they analyze and build abstract theories to understand their experiences. They have a scientific approach and function best in well-defined, structured environments. Unemotional and often more comfortable with things than people, they focus on uncovering accurate explanations.

Accommodators perceive concretely with their senses and feelings, and process actively. They are doing sensor-feelers. Active experimenters and pragmatic, they learn best from projects, back-home applications, and trying things out. They prefer practical application of learning. Result-oriented, they grab hold of experiences, make adjustments, frequently ignore theory, and start right in applying knowledge they accept as true.

A graphic comparison of Jung's and Kolb's styles with relevant instructional methodological approaches for each appears in table 4.

A PERSONAL PERSPECTIVE ON STYLE

It is not usually feasible or even advisable to ascertain students' styles by administering either the Myers-Briggs Type Indicator or Kolb's Learning Style Inventory. That does not mean, however, that you will not be able to assess their styles. While very likely you will not be able to assess the precise learning style of every student, you can generate a general but nevertheless fairly accurate impression when you anticipate that learners have different preferences and abilities, observe how students react in class, vary your methods so that different styles will be accommodated, offer choices in how they will learn, know their expectations, honor their prior knowledge and experience, and acknowledge their pressures and constraints.

Stylistic differences are all interrelated and in the long run provide you with direction in devising an integrated and individualized plan for delivering content and initiating experiential methods that cultivate reflection and foster relationship-building.

Although there is no direct correspondence between the theories of Jung and Kolb, a number of similarities and overlaps can be inferred. Extrapolating from these, I advance suggestions for planning and selecting methods to utilize for four styles of learning. Style 1 encompasses the ideas of Jung as they apply to sensors and Kolb as they apply to accommodators. Style 2 encompasses the ideas of Jung as they apply to intuitors and Kolb as they apply to assimilators. Style 3 encompasses the ideas of Jung as they apply to "thinkers" and Kolb as they apply to "convergers." Style 4 encompasses the ideas of Jung as they apply to feelers and to Kolb as they apply to divergers.

For style 1 students: explicitly plan a class using a clear, unambiguous structure with limits and goals carefully and explicitly stated. Proceed in a deliberate, step-by-step fashion, systematically adding new information to gradually approach a larger understanding. Permit a variety of activities, plan

Table 4. Comparative Learning Styles

	Jung Types	Approach		Kolb Types
Feeler	• Personal • Emotional • Responds to motives • Interested in harmony	*Group Process Humor Helping Appeal to heart*	Concrete Experiencer (CE)	• Receptive • Experience-based • Responsive to feelings • Involvement
Intuiter	• Synthetical • Imaginative • Abstract • Questioning • Interested in playing hunches and possibilities	*Creativity Challenges Patterns/themes Metaphors Independent discerning*	Abstract Conceptualizer (AC)	• Conceptual • Theory-oriented • Interested in abstractions
Thinker	• Organized • Analytical • Ordered • Skeptical	*Lecture Cause and effect Analysis Planning Organizing Appeal to head*	Reflective Observer (RO)	• Thinker • Tentative • Impartial • Reasoner • Analytical • Careful observer
Senser	• Here-and-now oriented • Action-focused • Doer • Interested in details and facts	*Projects Specifics Next steps Real life Concrete Firsthand experience Handouts*	Active Experimenter (AE)	• Pragmatic • Project-oriented • Application-focused • Responsible • Doer

for next steps, provide extra work, and make all the learning functional and practical. Give specific, brief, literal, and concrete instruction and develop active tasks. Appeal to their no-nonsense nature. Praise completion of successful projects and homework. Always relate content to real-life application. As much as possible, build in active firsthand experiences, simulations, and handouts. Be end-result- and application-oriented. Answer what-if questions. Formulate problems. Addressing how to apply learning is critical.

For style 2 students: be flexible, provide room for them to explore new ideas that are not explicitly preplanned. Encourage creativity in projects and discussions. Allow breathing space that permits time for their own input and an opportunity to synthesize and fantasize. Appeal to their creativity. Challenge them with mind teasers, puzzles, strategy games, and independent learning activities. Focus on patterns, themes. Ask open-ended, exploratory, and challenging questions. Allow for argument. Use and integrate the information into larger conceptual patterns. Metaphors are reveled in because they are ambiguous and invite inventive rumination. They excel at critical incidents. Having a capacity for being self-critical, they enjoy the opportunity to stray and dream up novel ideas. Why is crucial.

For style 3 students: define a structure that is emotionally neutral, relying on a low-key environment. Lecture in a logical, lucid manner, pointing out cause-and-effect relationships. Be orderly, well prepared, and thorough. Appeal to their intellectuality and rationality, their heads as opposed to their hearts. Inquisitive, they are distinguished by their intellectual curiosity. Content, particularly abstract ideas, is central. Be fair and praise their diligence and rationality. Reward accuracy. Be specific with expectations and highly organized. Provide opportunities to plan, analyze ideas, and critique theories. Socratic questioning, lectures, panel discussions, PowerPoint presentations, debates, and brainstorming appeal to style 3 learners. What, as opposed to how or why, is critical.

For style 4 students: atmosphere is everything. Create a warm environment that promotes intensive interaction, sharing of feelings and opinions. Appeal to their awareness, their sensibility, and their hearts. Mutual aid, group activities, and discussion are all welcome. Role play, sensitivity exercises, values clarification, fishbowl, psychodrama, storytelling, case studies, intensive open-ended journaling—all such expressive activities contribute to their engagement. Provide individual personal reactions. Stress common outlooks and capacities while at the same time stressing individuality. Attentiveness to process is key. Disclose personal information relevant to the topics under study. Use humor.

DOING WHAT COMES UNNATURALLY

Juggling four styles in one class is a daunting prospect. There is probably a dominant style among your student/practitioners that will determine your choice of approach. Likely the feelers, because of the profession they have chosen, will compose the largest segment of the class. That does not mean you cannot or should not use varying methods to appeal to the minority as well. As you need to be flexible and open, so do your students. Because something does not come naturally to them does not mean they cannot respond or perhaps enjoy an approach that disturbs their comfort zone.

It is probably wise not to limit oneself to what comes naturally in terms of your own style when teaching. Open yourself to varying notions. Try out alternate methods. Modify your techniques. Balance the rational and the emotional, the conceptual and the experiential. In other words, try at times to do what does not come naturally.

For those of you who incline most easily toward subject-area knowledge, to theory, to abstract conceptualization, and usually to lecture as a means of conveyance; who are highly structured and textbook-focused; who expect students to take prodigious notes and possibly memorize material; who ask closed-ended questions with pre-specified answers; shift gears. It is essential that students acquire mastery of theory and secure command of the content. Stimulating their curiosity, arousing their interest, however, is equally important. Get feedback directly from students, introduce into your repertoire a wider array of methods, experiment with them, open the door for shared opinions and points of view, pose open-ended questions.

For those of you with a rich repertoire of experiential methods, remember that it is imperative to relate experiential outcomes to the base line of the subject matter. Bear in mind that learning does not automatically accrue from participating in role plays, discussing cases, seeing movies, telling or listening to stories, drawing on art and photographs, or writing in journals. Getting the point—retention—is crucial to a firm grasp of the discipline. Buttress your presentation by making a concerted effort to organize material, to summarize content, to relate experience to theory, to connect the emotional to the empirical, to integrate it all with the expressed goal of the class and course.

The implication here is to balance content and process, lecture and expressive methods, teacher-centered and learner-centered methods. Be fluid, open. Incorporate a range of possible techniques into your repertoire.

Lesson Architecture

A good teacher is someone who can spark and kindle the fire of intellectual curiosity—and the learner believes it's a result of spontaneous combustion.

—ANONYMOUS

This remark says it clearly: the best teaching sets learners on their own path to discovery. Appeal to students' hearts as well as filling their heads; it is sustenance for their professional journey.

Effective, engaging, and enjoyable lessons do not happen automatically. They take effort. They demand attention to striking the right balance between content and process, to meeting the requirements of the curriculum and the distinctive needs of students. Every course is different. Every class is organic. Every group of students is distinctive. A tightly framed lesson leaves room for the unexpected and exceptional—a corollary to the apparent paradox stated earlier—structure frees you to be spontaneous. It affords room for you to weave teachable moments into the overall fabric of the lesson.

Curricula and syllabi are basically fixed, general, and inflexible. Without compromising the integrity of the prescribed content, a solidly designed lesson creatively customizes classes to reflect your particular expertise, preferences, and manner. At the same time it takes into account students' experience, strengths, and styles. Pre-reflection lesson planning—pulling it all together, in other words—is a kind of mental rehearsal. It focuses on desired changes in students, envisions the optimal conditions for creating a context for learning, and generates a strategy to intertwine process and content into a vibrant tapestry. Weaving it together calls for a self-conscious and conscientious effort.

THE LESSON PLAN

The lesson plan takes stock of the characteristics and conditions associated with you (personality, knowledge, skills, experiences, style), with students (receptivity, motivation, attitude toward the subject, style), with classroom milieu (number of students, physical environment, room temperature, acoustics), and with varied modes of instruction. It increases the likelihood of achieving greater student participation and optimizing learning. It makes teaching more stimulating and gratifying for both students and you.

A lesson plan arises from pre-reflection and buttresses both reflection-in-action, and reflection-on-action. It harnesses your ingenuity to coalesce a multitude of factors—goals, themes, patterns, assignments, exercises, and enhancement materials (e.g., handouts) into a coherent and unified presentation. The lesson plan plots a path through this complex terrain by synchronizing this panoply of variables.

A well-planned lesson enables you to integrate incidental learning events, make adaptations for spur-of-the-moment revisions, dwell longer on unfamiliar terrain, or move quickly past already mastered material. It also encourages self-reflection and creative forethought. It occasions a practice representation or simulation for the upcoming lesson.

In advance of formulating the new lesson, reflect on the previous one and then ask yourself: "What do I now want the students to know and to be able to do at the end of the lesson?" "How will I get them there?" "How will I be sure that they have arrived?"

COMPONENTS OF THE LESSON PLAN

The lesson plan is commonly comprised of six parts, each represented by a question: (1) *Who* are the students? (2) *Where* are they now? (3) *What* do you want them to know or do and *why*? (4) *How* do you intend to get there? (5) *How long* will it take? and (6) How will you know *when* you have arrived? These foundational questions give rise to additional ones: How does this particular lesson reflect the module, course, and syllabus? How does it connect with what came before? How does it segue into future lessons? What sequence will be followed? Beyond these more proximate foci of the lesson in terms of desired results, mull over the long-range prospect of what enduring understanding you want the student to have retained after the course is completed.

It is critical to determine desired outcomes. What should students know and be able to do? What provocative questions lead to big ideas? How will you know when students truly get the message? What is the evidence? How will themes and patterns be emphasized? How will you make learning both engaging and effective? Tease out priorities: What is essential to grasp deeply? What is secondary or tertiary? What is enduring?

When cultivating a lesson, keep in mind a few ideas. A large amount of your influence is indirect and/or tacit; therefore, it is best to *show* students skills in the same way that they are expected to employ them with their clients. Provide ample time and opportunity for students to integrate and practice these skills over several periods, so as to develop some confidence in their mastery. Students benefit when they grasp the meaning and organization of the whole before the discrete parts; so flow from the general to the specific when presenting theoretical material. When you build puzzlement, perplexity, and questioning into your lessons, students' critical thinking and deepened reflection are stirred and challenged. Major points presented at the beginning and at the end of the lesson are remembered by students more keenly than those presented in the middle.

SEQUENCE OF THE LESSON

The following lesson template, roughly based on sonata form, is a useful guide for you to thing about in designing each lesson:

Overture (Warm-up)
    Linking the class to previous class(es)
    Providing time to review reading assignments
    Revisiting leftovers from former classes
    Identifying current issues
    Transitioning to the present lesson
        Quotation
        Cartoon
        Puzzle
        Anecdotes
    Summarizing former themes

Exposition: (Body of Lesson)
    Selecting content emphasis
        Knowledge
        Skill
        Attitude/affect
    Choosing resources
        Handouts
        Videos/movies
        Case material
    Specifying three "musts" that must be covered
    Pinpointing methods based on students' learning styles
        Lecture
        Discussion
        Role play
        Journaling

      Debate
      Brainstorming, etc.
   Determining sequence

Coda: (Application to Practice)
   Recapitulating and summarizing
   Providing T.I.P.S. for transfer to client work
      Techniques
      Ideas
      Perspectives
      Skills
   Building a bridge to the next lesson

At the start of each class, encapsulate the lesson template into a brief outline to write on the board or project onto a screen. This procedure appeals to learners who are conceptual, pragmatic, and organized. They use it as a guide for note-taking and to gauge the flow of the lesson. A prototype outline appears below. Naturally it is customized to accommodate the special subject matter at hand, the phase of the course, the responsiveness of students, the goal and purpose of the particular unit of attention. The template as translated into an outline for students to view at the start of a class might appear as follows:

I.   Questions, Concerns, Comments
II   Themes from Previous Class
III. Brief Lecture, Videotape, Process Recording, etc.
IV. Case Presentation, Role Play, Movie Clip, Professional Tape, etc.
V.   Discussion of Theoretical Perspective
VI. T.I.P.S.

Alongside the outline, quotations follow as another thematic overture. Abstract learners appreciate this take on the content and readily absorb the meanings of the citations and their relevance to what is being studied.

    As a third component, cartoons are distributed capturing yet another version of the theme. Introducing each class with a carefully selected cartoon or two not only adds levity but supplies another pertinent angle on the material. Cartoons are more memorable than teachers. Humorous and familiar, they compress the essence of a lesson into a few concrete images. They have great appeal for those sensitive-style learners in the room.

    A further comment on outlines, quotations, and cartoons: each communicates the lesson's essential message in a different form, appealing to different learning styles. These procedures also set the tone for the day and provide an auxiliary cast on the lesson. They are chosen not only because they appeal to different learner styles, but because they liven up the lesson and stimulate students.

MORE ON LESSON SEQUENCE AND STRUCTURE

The overture consists of questions, concerns, and comments. Because transitions are so important, set time aside at the outset of each class to link the previous class to the present one, to intercept any residual vestiges or misunderstandings from the class before, to clarify any confusion about readings, to review homework, to expound on assignments, and to address any other concerns that may arise. Your lesson plan anticipates how transitions may occur as you shift from one focus to another in either content or method. Identifying themes from the previous class involves culling and underscoring three or four major ideas from previous meetings, readings, or assignments. Doing so generates momentum as it reinforces learning and draws attention to the principal constituents of former lesson(s). The exposition of the lesson concentrates attention on the lesson's principal emphasis—knowledge assimilation, skill development, or attitude change, as well as on techniques for its exposition— experiential exercises such as role playing, viewing videotapes or movies, or case presentations and critical incidents. The lesson's conclusion, or coda, is the synopsis of the lesson. T.I.P.S. denotes techniques, ideas, perspectives, and skills. Students are asked to name the lesson's major thrust and how it can be applied to their day-to-day practice. Seeds of a more professional stance are germinated. At the same time, it offers you a glimpse of what took root in students' minds and what did not. It helps you to assess the outcome of the lesson, which influences the plan for the subsequent class. It also provides an opportunity to direct students to resources—journal articles, books, TV programs, movies, Web sites, and so on—outside of class to augment the lesson. Unsurprisingly, it sometimes happens that the outline is not fully realized; however, more often than not, the intended thrust of the day has been accomplished, and connections to additional germane sources have been made. This structure permits teachable moments to be interlaced into the fabric of the lesson.

Concluding each class of a doctoral course devoted to the principles, processes, and pragmatics of teaching is a method called "mapping the lesson." Time is spent reviewing, analyzing, and critiquing each phase of the preceding lesson to retrospectively evaluate its clarity of focus, relevance of content, and suitability of techniques. Paralleling this approach, the concluding moments of a monthly faculty teaching seminar is called, appropriately, "sparks and ashes." It provides participants with the option to relate the triumphs, elevating moments, and "ahas" they experienced during the prior month while teaching. They are welcome to share letdowns and disappointments. The group members support, commend, and cheer colleagues on or commiserate and offer suggestions about ways to approach these situations differently.

You play a direct role in developing students' motivation and conceptual achievement by planning ways to involve them more fully in understanding instructional goals, providing conditions conducive to learning, and explaining to students what you are doing as the lesson unfolds. Draw attention to your shift from one form of instruction to another. For example, as you conclude a lecture, state that you are moving on to a role play, a case presentation, or a videotape. Doing so is functional. It prepares students in advance for any adjustments required of them—physically (e.g., rearranging chairs), intellectually (e.g., shifting gears), and emotionally (e.g., warming up). This procedure is beneficial when working with clients. Among other things, it opens channels of communication and reduces resistance. For yourself, noting your course of action and its results brings to the foreground those methods you might choose to avoid in the future because they fell flat, as well as those you might repeat because they succeeded.

RELEVANT METHODS FOR CONTENT DELIVERY

The diagram in table 5 depicts three fundamental domains of a lesson—cognitive, affective, and skill—their content bases, and selected methods best suited for their delivery.

Following are some versatile configurations for a lesson plan building on these domains, content bases, and relevant methods for effective presentation. They are similar in that they all systematically attend to the five or six

Table 5. Lesson Domain, Content, and Method

	Domain		
	COGNITIVE	AFFECTIVE	SKILL
Content	Knowledge base	Value base	Skill base
Methods	Lecture	Clarification	Role play
	Socratic questioning	Journaling	Recording
	Debate	Case presentation	Oral presentation
	Panel discussion	Brainstorming	Fishbowl
	PowerPoint	Storytelling	Demonstration
		Sensitivity exercises	Simulation

facets of the lesson plan advanced earlier in the chapter. They differ with respect to their emphasis—time, objectives, or themes.

The format shown in table 6 is particularly suited to aspiring teachers who require practice in monitoring the amount of time to devote to discrete segments of the lesson and its overall flow.

The template of table 7 places emphasis on goal formulation as the lesson's principal component, which guides it in a particular direction aimed at facilitating assessment of outcome.

The approach depicted in table 8 appeals to master teachers who consistently groom their lessons to improve delivery in conveying more encompassing core messages.

WHEN THINGS GO AWRY

The best-laid plans can go awry and do more frequently than we'd like to imagine. An illustration: one day a videotape was selected to show in a class

Table 6. Time-Focused Lesson Plan

Time	Goal	Duration	Content	Method/Activity	Purpose

Table 7. Goal-Focused Lesson Plan

Goal	Content	Method/Activity	Purpose	Assessment	Time

Table 8. Core Message Lesson Plan

Theme	Content	Method/Activity	Outcome	Next Steps

devoted to crisis intervention, a lesson depending on technical equipment. The moment came to show the tape, and of course the machine would not run. The tape could not be viewed. Calling for assistance from the technical staff, they finally arrived ten minutes later but were unable to fix it. The electric outlet was dead. After contacting administration, another room was located two floors above. Twenty-five students and I trudged to the elevator and up to the new room. Twenty more minutes elapsed, the equipment was set up, the tape installed. We were set. Good news, the tape worked. Bad news. As the tape began, another instructor and her class barged into the room. It was her regularly scheduled room. What next? We left the class but had no place to go. Dumbfounded, we clustered in the corridor for the duration of the class period. Students refused to accept an apology for such mayhem. Instead they insisted that they found the experience to be instructive. The real lesson was watching the "expert" handle an unexpected crisis.

In another example, I experimented with having students contract for their grades—one might choose a B+, for example. The agreement was that, if the student submitted a paper not warranting a B+, it would keep being returned for revision until a B+ was achieved. What initially seemed to be a nifty idea produced student resentment as well as a hugely increased workload. It was abandoned the next semester. A more dramatic example involved a total overhaul of a course syllabus as the result of the events of 9/11.

What is the point? The point is that even if you have done everything right, the lesson can still go astray. Thankfully, when students are invested, see you as concerned, are convinced of your good intention, and you deal directly and forthrightly with the issue at hand, a goof can turn into a gift.

An example of a different form of departure from an original lesson plan occurred in a course titled the Philosophy of Science. This intensively cerebral course, which depends on critical and out-of-the-box thinking, is offered immediately after an advanced statistics class, emphasizing quite different cognitive mindsets. Students tend to be intimidated, overwhelmed, and preoccupied by the previous quantitative material as they arrive in class. In order to help them to shift gears, redirect their energy, and allow time for decompression, puzzles were introduced to begin the class. The puzzles—spatial, language-based, mathematic, or analogic—go far beyond original expectations. Whether for individuals or groups, they break inertia and actually improve the lesson by stimulating unique ways of thinking, recruiting original ideas, and augmenting the topic at hand.

GUIDELINE QUESTIONS FOR PRE-REFLECTIONS

In pre-reflective planning, strive to concentrate your attention on some of these preparatory questions:

- How will you begin the lesson?
- Are your goals clear?
- Do your methods match the objectives?
- Does the lesson link to and augment previous material?
- Is there sufficient variety in presentation?
- Is there a logical sequence?
- Are focal points identified and highlighted?
- Are important points adequately reinforced?
- Is the organization clear?
- Is appropriate time allotted?
- Do you build in a formative check?
- Is your emphasis appropriate for the course at large?
- Will it hold students' attention? Yours?
- What resources advance further learning?
- Are verbal and nonverbal content integrated and complementary?
- What assignments enrich understanding?
- How will achievement be evaluated?
- Do I have at hand several concrete examples of larger concepts?
- Do I use concrete, everyday language?
- Do I incorporate nonverbal means (silence, pauses) to stress material?
- Are diagrams, graphs, case material available to facilitate explanation?
- How do I include anecdotes to break tension and support assimilation?
- Are transitions from one topic and from one method to another sound?
- How will I wind up the lesson?

PART III

Reflective Techniques

*Teaching means wearing a number of different hats,
sometimes piled on top of one another.*

—DR. SEUSS

CREATIVITY AND VARIATION in instructional methods are the key to learning. Dare to wear different hats to tap innovative resources to engage students fully—cognitively and emotionally—in their learning.

Six interdependent methods to advance relational acuity and reflective discernment—journaling, movies, storytelling, case/critical incident, photography and art, and role playing—are spotlighted in this section. These are resourceful means for making learning directly relevant to students from diverse backgrounds who have varied learning styles. Grounded in the common language of experience, they promote reflection and encourage relating. The methods intersect with one another, are complementary, and cohere. Use traditional methods such as lecture, but use them less. Experiment with these hands-on strategies. They anchor you as they catalyze students as doers and as seekers.

These six methods are vibrant, active, and truly student-centered. They go well beyond simply memorizing facts. They foster students' opening their minds to unfamiliar principles and viewpoints.

Students may have theoretical knowledge but require firsthand, step-by-step acquaintance of what it is like to face clients. The principal advantage to each and all these methods is that they transfer into practical application. All of them are modifiable for use with clients.

It has been repeatedly pointed out that there are many ways of knowing. Professional educational tends to rely on left-brain approaches of cognition—

logic—which often translates into a fixed and static pedagogy. Judicious choice of the assortment of methods described in this section appeal both to the left and right hemispheres. These methods are linked in that they can seamlessly bridge one method of instruction (e.g., lecture, story, movie) to another (e.g., discussion, role play, art). A case triggers a role play. A role play occasions a journal entry. A journal entry prompts a story. All stimulate discussion.

Journaling, movies, storytelling, case/critical incident, photography and art, and role playing provide authentic and realistic material. They nudge students into facing and mastering difficult concepts and constructs.

Because vantage points shift constantly as they unfold, an essential part of capitalizing on these inventive approaches is discussing, exploring, and evaluating their impact. Generalizing from the experience by extracting themes and meaning promotes successful application of the derived learning.

Keep in mind that lessons are more likely to be understood and remembered if presented through diverse entry points.

Consider these questions to guide you in the selection of experiential methods: How does this method fit into the way these particular students learn? What position does it hold in regard to the goals toward which you are working? What immediate and observable educational need does this particular method meet at this particular time? How does the method enhance reflection and relationships?

Writing for Insightful Reflection

We . . . write to heighten our own awareness of life . . .
to taste life twice, in the moment and in retrospection
. . . to be able to transcend our life and reach beyond it.

—ANAÏS NIN

Nin makes a strong point: gifts accrue from delving into one's innermost core through writing.

When I first wrote about the power of words and writing in the helping professions, I was criticized. Many believed that writing diluted the therapeutic process because it disengaged the writer from the immediate experience. But, of course, that's the point.

Writing provides a resource for gaining perspective, developing self-awareness, and integrating knowledge. It involves an array of senses—sight, touch, perhaps even the sound of a pencil scratch or the smell of wet ink. The very act of writing allows you to manipulate and wrestle with thoughts in special ways because it makes thoughts visible and tangible. It makes intentional and systematic your own as well as students' inquiry into learning and practice. Writing is a vehicle for self-study, self-reflection, and self-discovery. It is a valuable supplement to the teaching process, stimulating self-observation.

You and some of your students may be intimidated by the idea of putting thoughts down in black and white; it takes courage. Multiple benefits, however, accrue from the effort. This chapter highlights the multifaceted merits and flexible use of a few different platforms of writing for you as well as students. It offers an assortment of strategies to highlight its efficacy.

THE MERITS OF WRITING

Jung advocated writing as a tool to make sense of our experiences, of cause-and-effect relationships, of what is happening and why. It does so because representations of the right hemisphere are integrated with interpreting ones of the left. Writing helps us to figure out our own minds as well as access others'. Pulling back from the immediate situation, writing as self-study puts Dewey's and Schon's ideas of reflective thinking into concrete terms.

In all its forms, writing is an effective tool for observation and disclosure. It is not a substitute for, but rather an enhancement to interactive, person-to-person learning transactions. It is complementary *and* supplementary. It gives voice to students' and your own ideas, feelings, and patterns. It adds coherence to memories, thoughts, and intuitions. It facilitates communication, since sharing one's writing reduces the distance between students and each other, and between students and faculty. It provides a bridge in relationships, because open sharing with an audience cuts through barriers of solitude. In short, writing encourages students to think and reflect and invites them to articulate the outcome of doing so. A serendipitous advantage of writing is that it slows things down for mindful introspection.

Writing has incalculable impact on both you and your students. It invariably leads to deeper understanding and the integration of knowing, feeling, and doing. Employed in tandem with other techniques, and with sensitivity and discretion, it leads to remarkably candid self-analysis and honest reflection.

Restrictions of time limit the depth and breadth of exploration in face-to-face classroom encounters with students. Writing provides continuity to your work together and can be used in a variety of ways. Entries can be assigned to students or their free expression encouraged. Directed, structured process recording, semi-structured journal entry, or open-ended discursive narrative logs facilitate access to students' interpretations of their readings, client encounters, and personal prejudices. Writing can range from being somewhat mechanical and technical to being intensely expressive and fluid. It continues the momentum of your class work outside its formal structure. It sustains interest and focus in the learning process.

Writing can take many forms—concise outline, lengthy letter, essay, scattered phrases or words, note cards, letters to editors, blogs. Whatever system you arrive at, have students conclude with succinct encapsulations of their entries. The very way students express themselves offers a transparency of their learning process projected onto the page. Writing captures troublesome moments as well as positive and successful ones. It shows how students apply learning to practice and how their practice fuels learning.

Writing documents students' facing new or unusual circumstances. It helps you and them to identify gaps in knowledge and skill, but also locate their strengths and capacities. It systematically addresses weighty questions: How do I make sense of what I am seeing? Of what I am doing? Why don't I understand what seems so apparent to my colleagues?

Lecture, reading, discussion, all are useful ways of conveying content. Unrecorded, however, they may lose intensity and staying power. Left simply to memory, their import may fade. When time and energy is dedicated to mulling them over, to musing, to pondering, to *writing* them down, enormous gains ensue.

INTRODUCING THE PRACTICE OF WRITING

Introduce the idea of writing in initial classes. Explain its purpose. Develop guidelines for the particular form of writing for that particular course. Below you will find suggestions for three forms of writing: process recording, semi-structured journals, and open-ended journals. Deadlines for submission for each will vary according to the respective approach. For example, certain skills are best developed incrementally, therefore writing tasks are spaced accordingly. Whatever method is employed, ask that in their first entry students record impressions, questions, omissions, concerns, or whatever else comes to mind about the initial class, about writing itself. This early use of writing familiarizes students with the process. Writing provides an incisive perspective into students' situations because, progressive and cumulative, it furnishes instant participation and allows both of you to examine progress at different junctures in the teaching process.

Periodic and conscious reexamination of writing by you and students facilitates meaning-making and reflection. Information is not knowledge; it is transformed into knowledge when a shift is made to higher levels of cognitive and affective understanding. Committing ideas to paper is a valuable means for such transformation to occur.

PROCESS RECORDING

Process recording is a special and singularly important type of writing. It is a timely, formal, and firsthand account of a current, dynamic transaction between students and clients. Introspective and analytical, it is a circumscribed form of writing. Deliberately structured, it organizes thinking and reflection on themes, theories, and skill sets as they pertain to contact with clients.

Introducing this all-too-familiar form of writing usually elicits sighs and grunts from students. They cringe at the amount of time it consumes. Yet process recording provides an invaluable means to evaluate and conceptualize interactions with clients. A standardized process-recording outline, described below, introduced at the start of a course, encourages students' conceptualization of their practice at all stages—preparation, assessment, intervention, and outcome evaluation. It is time devoted as much to thinking and reflecting as to writing. When looking back, students find newfound merit in what previously had been for them a mindless exercise.

Students are counseled to listen carefully to and to concentrate on each interaction between themselves and clients in order to accurately record what occurs. Immediately after meeting with clients, students are instructed to conjure an image, recall the voice, gestures, and posture of clients to jog memory. Jotting down key words helps recall. Attending carefully to what they see and hear is itself a form of reflection. Writing helps students to be active rather than passive observers. A vehicle for review and assessment on their practice as it unfolds, process recording promotes organized and disciplined thinking.

Process recording also promotes relational collaboration between you and students in identifying learning needs and expectations and tracking progress toward achievement of educational goals. An organizing medium, reading entries in advance of class can influence your selecting it for classroom review. It provides a concrete means for assessing student competence in reaching goals set early in the semester. It also synchronizes classroom learning with field practice.

Process recording is not merely a verbatim transcription recollected from memory or a static retrospective reconstruction of interpersonal exchange. It is a mode of methodical observation and analysis that enables you to evaluate outcomes in integrating theory into practice. Its ultimate benefit is the development of a reflective practitioner (Schon, 1983).

Process recording imparts concise and ordered accounts of students' work leading to case material and critical incident content pertinent for illustrative classroom exchanges. It makes evident students' unique ways of thinking and problem-solving. Although structured, uniqueness emerges from the individualized way students employ it.

Five-Part Outline

You can adjust this suggested outline at varying points to emphasize your specific learning and educational purposes. It may be narrative and discursive or columnar and brief. Discourage excessive detail or extraneous information. Process recording plainly documents service, identifies needs, forms a basis for intervention planning, presents a vehicle for tracking progress, and for sharing information with other students and with you.

The special feature of this distinct five-part outline is its being both process- and product-oriented (Fox & Gutheil, 2000). Providing a channel to focus students' critical abstract thinking (process) about their interaction (more process) with clients, it inspires higher levels of abstraction and critical analysis. It then documents a student's work, crisply and coherently (product).

The outline's components are not actually discrete entities. They overlap. You may choose to have the components integrated into one narrative, or to separate them out into headings. Five critical elements of practice are integrated into this framework: preparation, intervention, questioning and analysis, evaluation, and planning next steps.

In the five-part outline example from box 1, an excerpt from a student's actual case process recording of Mr. and Mrs. W accompanies each subsection.

THE SEMI-STRUCTURED JOURNAL

Another—possibly more scholarly—form of writing is the structured, guided, or topically focused journal. It documents how students wrestle with facts and ideas presented in readings, in lectures, in field visits, and internship trainings rather than with clients per se. Less structured than process recording but more formal than an open-ended journal described later, it focuses on how students grapple with theory, perspectives, and issues. While it incorporates a modicum of the subjective, it concentrates on students' responses to external sources rather than internal ones. It usually requires interpretations of texts, succinct reactions to articles, encapsulations of guest lectures, and so on. Pose a question or identify a series of topics related to a particular module under study to guide students in their entries. This type of writing summarizes, analyzes, and critiques what they are learning. Entries relate to their applying the learning in their practice. Different from the other two forms of writing proposed, each a form of discourse with you or with other students, students dialogue, as it were, with authors, lecturers, and experts. Entries keep students centered on specific subject matter.

Students make entries on a regular basis, such as once or twice a week. Entries respond to the general guidelines below and are intended to relate to the topic of the lesson, reading, and so forth:

Description

Keep a weekly journal. Its focus is to assist you to bridge theory and practice. This notebook records your reactions to readings, class lectures, and training activities. It explains how you connect them to your work with clients. No summary of the reading is necessary; rather, react to the readings, express your opinions, and identify how they have informed your practice.

The final entry involves two steps. First, read through the semester's entries and review them for recurring themes. Search for connections and relationships. Underline these along with words or phrases that reappear.

Box 1   Recording Outline

I. Preparation and Purpose

Prior to client contact, record the rationale for your contact, key thoughts, aims, and plans for the contact and potential obstacles or pitfalls. Include methods to be used, data to be obtained, preliminary assessment formulations, issues for focused attention, and possible resistance to be faced. Some guideline questions include:

- Am I clear about my direction?
- What would be the preferred outcome?
- Do I have sufficient information and resources?
- What preliminary arrangements need to be made to enhance the exchange?

Example: "Marital difficulty. Ms. W comes alone. Totally reluctant to explore relationship. Need clearer light on interaction and husband. Doubts self, husband, me. Preemptively seeks a divorce. Where from here?"

II: Intervention

Describe the ebb and flow of the contact, including the verbal and nonverbal activity. Summarize what occurred interpersonally during your client contact, noting the responses and activity of both of you. Compile observations, including unique and unusual factors, cultural variables, and critical analysis. Include direct quotes to individualize and highlight significant elements. Some guideline questions are:

- How did the contact begin and end?
- What changed?
- What decisions were made?
- What tasks were accomplished?

Example: "Mrs. W responded well. More frank. Recommended couple counseling. Mrs. W herself suggested inviting Mr. W to a session. Offer an eight-week open contract to them."

III: Thoughts and Analyses

Articulate your spoken and unspoken thoughts and reactions to clients and examine your own and clients' functioning. Include consideration of client strengths, capacity, motivation, as well as impressions regarding the nature and quality of the helping endeavor. Pay attention to significant patterns and themes that emerge. Critically evaluate the interface of your activity with clients' progress. Important questions include:

- What did I learn about myself and my knowledge and skill application?
- What do I need to know more about in terms of the client(s) and ways of interacting?

- What was particularly difficult for me or the client(s)?
- If I were to do it over again, what would I do differently?

Example: "Mr. and Mrs. present. I was too impatient, moved too quickly—slow down. Both bring crucial past family baggage. Unpack it; introduce genogram next time."

IV: Overall Evaluation and Next Steps

Specify "use of self," knowledge, and skills used to reach the stated purpose, to tailor the interaction to clients' expressed and special needs. Reflect on and assess how appropriate, realistic, and effective your strategies for intervention were. Some guideline questions are:

- How effective was the joining of method of intervention to the needs of the client(s)? What interventions were successful?
- Which ones did not work? Why?
- Where am I in all this?

Example: "Went quite well. Mr. and Mrs. W intrigued by genogram. Insights for them and me into repeating patterns. Genogram good idea. Stick with it. Highlight the present. Interpret and interrupt repetition of prefigured modes."

V. Questions

The process recording concludes with specific questions and issues to be addressed regarding both students' and clients' needs. These questions may address specific concerns about the client, the student, or the interaction, or may relate to application of theory and special techniques. These questions offer a way of brainstorming, playing with novel ideas, reframing impressions, alternating perspectives, and making hunches. They provide valuable case material to be incorporated into classroom discussion.

Summarize any consistent ways you reacted to assignments, to clients, and so on. You may discover insights in this rereading that you overlooked in weekly entries. Record a meta entry reflecting back on the process of journaling up to this point.

Second, create an illustration using art, photographs, graph, time line, or some other nonverbal form of expression to portray your insights in the process of learning captured in the journal. Briefly describe what the illustration represents and how and why you chose it. It can take the form of a collage, a map, a timeline, a symbolic diagram, or anything you choose.

Format

Each journal should be typed, approximately two to three pages in length.

Schedule

The journal will be collected twice during the semester.

Grading Criteria

Range of content, crispness and quality of writing, accuracy, thoroughness, originality, and conceptualization.

One Short Illustration

"After reading chapter 11, I realize that I was totally off-base in my work with Ms. A. I really didn't understand the full impact of surviving all kinds of awful experiences. It never happened to me. It shed some light for me on what it was like. I cried at some of the stories, but I thought it (the chapter, I mean) was very helpful in seeing what it is like to have those terrible things happen. Ideas about how to work with my clients who have lived through suffering gave me guidance and direction."

Some teacher/practitioners have students read aloud from their journals during class. Reading them first and selecting relevant passages works better. When students deliver their journals, draw from them in a non-constrained and creative way. For example, with their prior agreement, you might read a selection from them anonymously at the beginning of class as background, concentrate on them exclusively, or not refer to it at all. You might select portions of it to discuss further or put it aside to peruse at another time.

Note cards provide a variation of this method. For example, on 3 x 5 cards students can capture summaries of reading assignments; develop questions to raise in class; identify reactions they want to share with you or with the entire class; link theory and research to individual experience; or advance opinions about reading, lectures, role plays, and so on. This offers an effective medium for stimulating discussion. It also allows you to pinpoint and thereby clarify misunderstandings and correct misconceptions. Whichever method you choose, request a culmination entry in which students summarize all the previous entries, connect them to lessons derived from the class, and provide a critical appraisal of their own learning. It offers a memorable closure to the course and a tangible record of their progress over time. A later chapter provides examples of how students in their journals map their most significant learning experiences.

THE OPEN-ENDED JOURNAL

An open-ended journal lends itself to a stream-of-consciousness method for students to subjectively sort things out. Spontaneous and free-flowing, entries are a springboard for students to reprise and recognize rational as well as intuitive resources. While words can conceal as well as reveal, students, particularly in advanced seminars, honestly and openly weave their own personal thread through the fabric of their practice experience. Very often, paradoxically, for those students having little tolerance for ambiguity, the spontaneous flow of thoughts or feelings provides impetus for less constrained expression. Their journals provide new insights into themselves and into their practice, anchoring new learning as it consolidates an overall synthesis of personal and professional self.

Here, students invest much of their selves, making it difficult for you to grade in traditional fashion. Doing so, in fact, is counterproductive. It impedes and constrains free and honest expression. To maximize its effectiveness as a highly unique and individualized means for self-reflection, avoid grading them in the usual sense. Rather, make marginal comments or endnotes. Open-ended logs are not recommended for required classes; rather, reserve their use for small, advanced, elective ones. This method facilitates students expressing innermost thoughts leading toward the discovery of qualities or deficiencies they may not yet be aware of. Taking time to look at themselves, at what they are doing, and what they are learning stimulates critical thinking as well as affective resonance. It documents growth. Open-ended writing is intensively introspective, narrative rather than analytic. It is, in a manner of speaking, students' dialogue with themselves.

Introduce open-ended journals by saying something like:

> An open-ended journal is a running account of your subjective stance, paving the way for inward mindfulness and inward attention.
>
> Write in the first person.
>
> Take time. Stick with it. When you step forward and press onward, the journal is freeing and illuminating.
>
> No formal rules or formulas apply. Put aside ordinary requirements and restrictions associated with grammar, syntax, and organization.
>
> There are neither right nor wrong ways of doing it. Likewise, there are no limits, no restraints. Design and redesign your journal process to work for you.
>
> Remain flexible and adaptable, remembering that the journal is better when it is not forced. Exerting pressure on yourself to maintain it discourages you from fully and honestly expressing what is truly going on in you as you write. It is not intended to be judged by you, by me, or by anyone else.

Open-ended logs often result in new revelations. One student wrote:

> To be honest, I really didn't know quite what I was doing until I jotted it down, put it aside for a while, wrote about it, and then reviewed it at a later time. As I undergo things, it takes time for it to sink in. I didn't want to do this in the first place, but I find that writing, almost randomly, then thinking about it later brings more appreciation and understanding of where I am coming from. Things that were not obvious to me, like totally ignoring clients when they talk about their fears. When I write and re-examine it later, it becomes more apparent to me that this is my issue, not theirs. I don't know if there would be another way to get it.

Another student wrote:

> I feel self-conscious and stupid. I try to say the right thing, avoid making mistakes, but invariably am unhappy with what I say to clients. To me, everyone else in class seems to know exactly what they are doing. Not me. I am realizing that it is exactly my rigidity and fear of making mistakes creating the very dilemma that I beat myself up for. Writing this, I'm beginning to recognize how much I interfere myself, with my more natural way of interacting with people. Instead of being open and listening to clients, I'm busy worrying about me and what is the right thing to say. Today with J, I followed hunches, allowed myself to be more intuitive and not be so concerned about the correct textbook ideas. I actually made a joke. Maybe being more natural, less neutral, less involved in myself than in them, is the better way to go. It is funny, no pun intended, that when I lightened up, made a humorous remark that J snickered at, I was encouraged, and felt competent, in tune with him and with me. Oh, please let it continue.

All these forms of writing—process recording, semi-structured journals, and open-ended journals—foster students' movement toward stages of development and higher order thinking as described by Kolb (1984).

WAYS TO USE WRITING

Forms of writing suggested in this chapter enable students to learn about the fine points of practice through detailed examination of their own performance, as well as hearing about others'. Especially in large classes, with limited time, writing breaks down the anonymity, making your relationship with students, and their relationship with each other, more personal. Simultaneously, writing fosters an appreciation of the relevance and application of theory. Sharing journals and process recording in classes leads to real peer review and cogent appraisal. Contributions in class are voluntary—seeks students' permission in advance to share entries, even anonymous ones.

To compensate for the limits that size and time impose, and because it is not possible for every student to contribute, at semester's end in one advanced class, each student prepares a two-page abstract from his or her semi-structured journal entries and makes enough copies to circulate to every member of the class. Consistent feedback from students over the years attests to these abstracts as constructive reference points for preparing for school and professional and state credentialing examinations. They serve as valuable reference points to consult when working with unfamiliar case situations in their practice settings.

As another example, every student in a small clinical seminar is required to make an oral case presentation. A week prior to this presentation, they submit to fellow students for their advance perusal a selected portion from one recent process recording, an annotated bibliography, and a discussion agenda, along with other material as described earlier. At class it is reviewed in depth. Students learn from each other's struggles and achievements and feel supported because they are not alone. Such pertinent written material goes beyond the textbook and makes the classroom come alive.

WRITING FOR YOURSELF

Writing is beneficial for you as well. It assists you in efforts to individualize students, select appropriate methods, appeal to differing styles, and create viable and appealing educational plans. It enables you to refine particular techniques and to review the effect of your instruction. It offers a rich opportunity to carry on a written, as well as verbal, dialogue with others in the same position or with more seasoned professionals. Experienced faculty find writing to be an advantageous means to reenergize themselves. As you play with ideas and concepts, the reflection induced by writing extends time devoted to issues arising from class and makes connections between personal beliefs, philosophy, happenings in the classroom, content, and so on. If you are able, find time immediately following the class to jot down an appraisal, impression, and/or critique of it. It is a constructive point of departure, a moment to mull over the class while it's fresh in your mind. It highlights the effectiveness of your delivery, takes stock of student immersion, and capitalizes on increased awareness to attune subsequent lessons the next time around. A former colleague, now deceased, recorded each and every one of his classes over a thirty-year span. He professed that doing so contributed to his repeatedly being lauded as an outstanding teacher. It allowed him to extract portions of it as he mentored novice teachers.

In her compelling book, *A Life in School: What the Teacher Learned* (1996), Jane Tompkins—referring to getting a grip on a new way of teaching—comments:

> Because I was doing this experimenting alone, without colleagues who'd taken similar risks, and had no way to compare my experience to the experiences of others, I needed some way to come to terms with what I was doing. I needed some way to make sense of experiences that were overpowering in their intensity. . . . This kind of teaching seemed to require a new kind of writing, a form that would reflect the spasmodic, concentrated quality of the experience, its precariousness, the constant sense of teetering on the brink that accompanied me from day one of that course and during most of my experimental courses, only letting go of me now and then.

Writing about your own teaching events is one of the best ways to give new meaning to your professional life. It also enables you to check yourself, as did Tompkins. What did I set out to accomplish? What kind of interaction occurred with the students? Did anything unusual happen? Did I do anything novel and with what results? If I taught the lesson again, what would I do differently? Did I discover anything new about myself? Overall, how effective was I? What more should I attend to? What requires more work? What were the most and the least successful parts of the lesson? Writing is an excellent tool for discernment. Clustering is another helpful technique.

CLUSTERING

Developed by Gabriele Rico (1983), clustering is a form of creative writing that can be freeing for you as well as for students. It helps you to contact inner process and gain self-awareness by accessing memories, freeing emotions, and capturing forgotten experiences.

An extemporaneous method of open-ended writing, clustering is akin to free association. Actually shaping an experience, it is an approach that forms and structures the confusion that sometimes characterizes our inner and outer world, especially when faced with an impasse or a dilemma. A form of brainstorming, it is a nonlinear activity that generates ideas, images, and feelings around a stimulus word. It can be seen as a process of moving to higher levels of abstraction and conceptualization. Beginning with a nucleus word and spilling off other words and phrases at random, complex images and emotional qualities associated with them become clear, leading to a pattern and organization of meaning not originally perceived. Patterns and themes emerge.

To start, on a blank page circle a chosen stimulus word or phrase that comes to mind. Let your mind flow and write down other words that you associate with it, each in its own circle that radiates from the first. Connect

the circles with lines. Start again when you have a new or different association. If it does not flow in any particular order, let each association find its
own place. Be receptive to what comes. Don't censor. When you have
exhausted this playful association, suspend your circling. Begin to write a
paragraph. You will be amazed at what comes together, at how the most troublesome thoughts can turn out to have unexpected depth and resonance. A
schematic of a blank cluster can be seen in figure 1.

While clustering can be undertaken privately, it is helpful to develop one
publicly for yourself as a vehicle to crystallize an idea to students. It's very
revealing for students to witness your own process in action (Schon, 1987).
Speak aloud as you refine, revise, and erase the cluster on the board and
strive to produce a lucid paragraph.

In a class devoted to psychoanalytic theory and practice, students had as
much difficulty getting the concept of transference as I had in articulating it.
As an impromptu gesture, believing it would be helpful, the word *transference*
was written on the board. The cluster that materialized in class (see figure 2)
resulted in a plausible explanation.

Starting from the word *transference*, the cluster expanded in seven directions, each with very different types of associations, until the sixth direction
led to a blank, ending the process. The translation of the cluster into a definition of transference led to this statement: "Transference is psychoanalytic

Figure 1 Blank Cluster

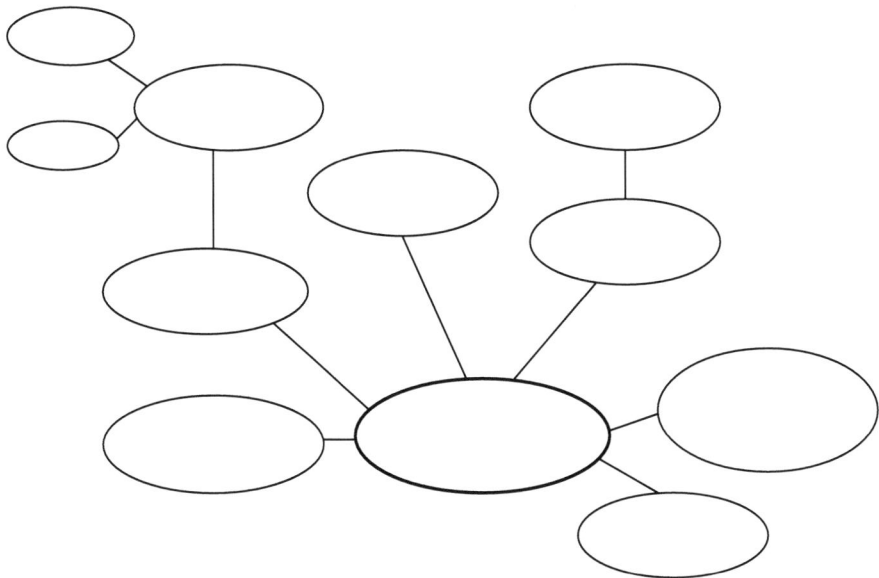

Figure 2 Clustering Transference

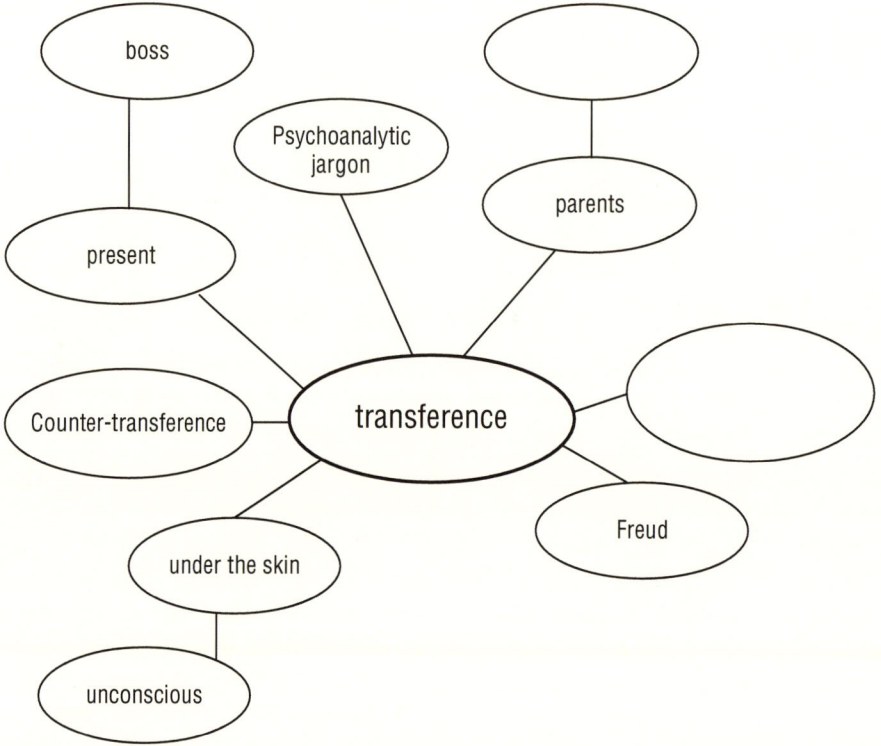

jargon for a Freudian concept, explaining a person's uncanny, 'under the skin' response to a person in the present, duplicating one from the past that appropriately belongs usually to one's parents. Countertransference is the helper's transference."

CO-DOCUMENTATION

Yet another writing method involves co-documentation. In this method students and you jointly agree at the outset of a course to author observations and interpretations over its duration. Presupposing that students have responsibility equal to yours for their learning, each of you assumes a complementary, different, yet essential role in coordinating and furthering the learning process as it unfolds in the moment. Independent versions of events are then compared to each other, which permits openly resolving differences, moving past impasses, examining concerns, modifying techniques, designing better ways to connect and communicate, forestalling setbacks, and affirming and reinforcing positive gains. Co-documentation provides evidence that you have impact and play a central role in the educational endeavor. It acknowledges students' skills, developing expertise and unique ways of perceiving and approaching situations.

Co-documenting parallels eliciting feedback, outlined in chapter 13, on role playing. It closely resembles mapping, described in detail in chapter 12. Its instantaneousness, timeliness, and continuity progressively kindles reflection and invigorates relationship-building.

ADVANTAGES OF WRITING

You may be wondering, with all the paperwork you already have, how to find the time or inclination either to read students' journals or to undertake yourself the various forms of writing presented in this chapter. They can at first seem overly time-consuming and burdensome. The advantages of writing, however, are more than fringe benefits. Writing helps students and you in profound ways. Some advantages of writing bear repetition, and others should be more clearly explicated. Writing encourages a stance of inward attention, of mindfulness; it develops a degree of comfort in self-observation and self-reporting; fosters alternative ways to approach things; establishes a sense of competence in being able to discipline and express yourself; leads to incisive self-reflection, especially when entries are reviewed over time; unfreezes thinking, making possible reinforcement of movement and change; and provides continuity during semester, summer, and other breaks.

An added bonus of writing is that it increases students' incentive and facility in writing per se. Its major attribute is that it can provide a before/after picture of the teaching process. It brings a sense of order and progression and highlights moments of decision. Particularly at the end of the semester, although at any interval along the way, it provides tangible documentation of progression in learning. It charts your impact, growth, and development as a teacher as well as students' movement toward professional mastery.

Movies: Media as Message

All media as extensions of ourselves serve to provide new and transforming vision and awareness.

—MARSHALL MCLUHAN

Media are powerful and creative instruments for stimulating motivation, arousing interest, and sustaining engagement in the educational process. McLuhan stresses the importance of vision in the broadest sense. Movies enhance and enrich the learning atmosphere as they depict universal themes and compel attention to essential interactions. Making visual the radiance of humanity, media unify the learner and teacher in mutual and mindful reflection.

Movies constitute one among many forms of media—including music, television shows, and literature—available for you to enliven lessons, to provide variety in class presentations, to augment conceptual frameworks, and to help your students better understand themselves, their clients, and the transactions between them. Movies can shed new light on themes, situations, and dilemmas students face daily. They can also cast into the foreground themes, situations, and dilemmas with which students have no previous firsthand acquaintance. Movies enhance deepened reflection. They endow lessons with added value. This chapter suggests movies suitable for use in courses in family treatment, teaching, and clinical practice. It focuses on the compelling nature of films and offers some guideposts for considering and selecting movies for your own courses.

MOVIES' ATTRIBUTES

Popular culture engages us with the world. Students are exquisitely attracted and attuned to visual stimulation. Portraying some of the most basic issues in human existence, movies can prompt students to take a more thoughtful look at the dynamics influencing clients and their environment. Such portrayal becomes an indelible lesson. "Moving pictures" are "moving" in a number of respects. They are active. They are compelling. They touch an emotional chord. They move students toward lively discussion. They move, supplement, and augment textual and case material. Movies poignantly capture relevant issues in the human condition—such as the suffering of physical illness and its consequences as portrayed in *Lorenzo's Oil*, the emotional isolation of a family as shown in *Ordinary People*, the tumult depicted in *Babe*, the question of mental illness as seen in *Don Juan DeMarco*, and clinicians' angst as in *Equus*. Watching films, replaying segments, and freezing action at carefully selected points encourages weighty reflection and discussion.

Movies visually and strikingly illustrate sensitive, nuanced, or difficult topics that elude verbal expression. They build on continuity of theme, and make the invisible visible as they create dramatic impact. Movies evoke emotional resonance. They transmit the challenges inherent in all forms of relationships and, as with other forms of art, make more easily accessible and easier to fathom complex psychological and philosophical subject matter.

Although there are professionally focused commercial videos and television shows that depict the helping process, movies, especially classics, better portray an array of themes—guilt, anger, fear, love, longing, absence, betrayal, and so forth—in ways that advance critical thinking and reflective pondering. They offer a wide range of possibilities for individual introspection and group deliberation.

Granted, there is a well-known tendency for Hollywood to distort reality and to perpetuate stereotypes, depict extremes, simplify complexities, and include only those details relevant to the plotline. Movies, however, when carefully chosen and discriminatingly used, deliver vivid, concrete, and memorable images that anchor learning.

Bringing popular culture, namely movies, into the classroom does not diminish an intellectual or professional focus; rather, drawn upon with care, they enhance both. Not mere entertainment, even though enjoyable, movies tap into emotions through identification and catharsis. They speak to students in a familiar language. Since teaching is itself an art form, a craft, what better way to boost a lesson than through artistic expression. Consider ways to incorporate movies into your coursework as a means to take advantage of their unique ability to conjoin emotion and reason, command attention, engage viewers, and raise consciousness.

Mixing reality with fantasy, fact with fiction, movies generate emotionally powerful responses and potentially healing reactions. They provide a view into others' lives. They give us access to greater understanding about ourselves, our families, our siblings—indeed, all of our relationships. They have special advantages. Students get the impression that they are actually present to the events. All students witness the same phenomenon at the same time from which to generate discussion. It's possible to play and replay segments to prompt feedback, clarify a point, invite interpretations, and capture the essence of a scene. You do not need to depend on one student's case presentation or your own recitation, since a movie can offer a plethora of possible angles on a situation. Movies provide a safe avenue to introduce unlikely or painful situations. Instant replay makes it possible to review certain interactions over and over again to underpin main points. Movies offer a variety of strategies and skills for looking at oneself, at others, at the world, and at the practice endeavor.

THE IMPACT OF MOVIES

Encapsulated here are sketches of a few movies with basic tactics for selecting, reviewing, and dissecting them. Like cases and stories, movies put forward human struggles that warrant reflection. Highlighted are the potent effects of engaging in a *process* of penetrating portrayed scenes, examining the *product* of such involvement, and ultimately, *introspecting* about their overall effect and meaning.

Movies should neither be the total class focus nor occupy the entire time. Rather, they are intended as grist for the learning mill. Supplementary and complementary, they are a stimulus, enhancement, or enrichment strategy to the conceptual foundation of your lesson. There is no assurance that as a result of watching a movie, or many movies for that matter, that your students will learn. What you decide to show depends on the particulars of your course, the individual lesson, students' styles of learning, and what makes the best sense at that juncture in the semester.

Situations in the movies may not exactly duplicate students' own current circumstances, or those of clients. Nevertheless, they offer for consideration a range of possible ways characters confront painful, overwhelming, and disheartening circumstances. They open students' minds to an array of alternative possible strategies for grappling with such distress. Movies also inspire students with upbeat episodes displaying the constructive and empowering nature of characters' fortitude and resilience.

GUIDELINES FOR SELECTING MOVIES

Make sure you preview movies before assigning or showing them. Determine their appropriateness. Assess their impact. Estimate if their messages can be deciphered. Estimate in advance the reaction to controversial content. Explain your reason for selecting them and showing them at a particular time.

As you preview a movie, ask yourself: Is it realistic? Is the message clear? Does it fit the lesson? Is it accurate? Does it allow students to experience a situation in which they haven't been, perhaps couldn't imagine? Does it create a strong impression? Does it allow students to project themselves into the action? Is the timing for viewing apt? Does it contribute substantially to the learning?

Anticipating in this way, beyond the appeal of the movie, sets both your and their minds to a relevant frame of reference. It bridges the gap between the orderly, staid milieu of the classroom and the intricate, complex world of practice.

MOVIES IN THREE DISCRETE CLASSES

Movies imitate life in depicting the tension between letting go and moving on, casting away what's old and grabbing hold of what's new. More often than not, our tendency is to go to an extreme in dealing with memories, ideas, relationships, feelings, and, yes, even dreams. Trouble arises when the old may be abandoned or the new launched without consideration of the consequences of doing so. Reflection aids in discriminating between choices that may end up as either hurtful and perhaps dangerous or ones that are healthy and constructive.

Watching how characters in the movies invent new directions and take unfamiliar paths suggests options for your students to undertake a similar stance. Watching how represented clients, practitioners, and educators bungle their way through, succeed, or fail kindles fascination and exploration. Recognize the need for direction. Anticipate problems.

Distribute handouts before class to direct attention to particular enactments and to clarify difficult material. Doing so ultimately enhances discussion. For example, provide a handout explaining the basics of adrenoleukodystrophy (ADL), before viewing *Lorenzo's Oil*, a movie about a boy with the untreatable condition and his parents' adoption of an unproven therapy in order to save him. Questions distributed in advance draw students' attention to certain aspects you seek to emphasize.

General questions might be: What did you learn from this movie? Was there something you did not understand? Did the events portrayed ring true? How did the movie connect with your reading? How did the movie resemble or differ from your practice perspective?

Movies in a Family Therapy Course

In a course I teach dedicated to family therapy, movies occupy a prominent place. Drawing from a mélange of didactic lectures, class discussion, and experiential exercises—but largely on movies and videotapes—the course focuses on providing an overview of family systems and theories of intervention. Various family forms (single-parent, separated, divorced, remarried, adopted, gay and lesbian, as well as families of diverse cultural and racial background) are studied. Also considered are the diverse range of dynamics and themes that characterize families in crisis, families dealing with trauma, families within the larger social context. Movies offer a venue for so broad a spectrum of issues and problems.

There are few movies depicting happy families. (*Father of the Bride* and *Meet Me in St. Louis* are two examples.) Most movies show families in the midst of crisis or tragedy. Dealing or *not* dealing with the painful and disruptive aftermath of crises of one sort or another—divorce, chronic illness, natural disaster, suicide, trauma, domestic violence—are movies' more typical focal point.

The family crises that occur episodically during a lifetime are often presented in an abbreviated timeframe in movies. Calamities occur, as in *A River Runs Through It* and *A Death in the Family*; loved ones die, as in *Terms of Endearment*; dreadful illness intrudes, as it happens in *Stepmom*; and families divorce, the central focus of *Kramer vs. Kramer*. Suicide profoundly affects an entire family, as it does in *Ordinary People*. The different members react to it in different, strange, and even contradictory ways. Guilt over failure to recognize or respond to the warning signs, shame associated with a deep sense of failure, fear of being blamed are movingly portrayed. *Ordinary People* captures how different family members grapple with emotions that surface when a family member kills himself. It shows further how such events frequently result in the total dissolution of family unity and peace.

To Kill a Mockingbird, *A Time to Kill*, and *The Burning Bed* all display the horror of rape as it devastates, infuriates, and incites individual victims as well as their mothers, fathers, and siblings. These movies illustrate the various ways people—traumatized, humiliated, stung—react to their sense of violation and loss of control. Some wallow in grief and resentment. Some mobilize their anger and distress. Some get past their doubts and if-onlys. Some exact revenge.

Crises also provide heightened opportunity to make choices about how to rebound. Interestingly enough, they often catapult families into reevaluating or reshaping the typical ways of relating that may have contributed to the seriousness of the crisis in the first place. Look at the parents (Nick Nolte and Susan Sarandon) in *Lorenzo's Oil*, consider the mother (Cher) in *Mask*, or think about the families portrayed in *Babe* and *What's Eating Gilbert Grape*. Crises, in other words, can make for decisive, deliberate, and positive change.

Clearly, there's more to the family than meets the eye. There are all sorts of families. All sorts of cultural factors, traditional rituals, styles, and forms. Movies create a multitude of images of the family. By exploring the whole gamut of family life, movies deeply affect our notions of how our own families work and suggest, sometimes explicitly and sometimes implicitly, what they should look like.

How can movies help students get in better touch with the impact of their own families as well as with clients' families? Movies go beyond simply showing stories that students can relate to. They show how the varying experiences of the patterns, functions, and relationships in families depicted offer a deeper insight of what factors underlie family dynamics. They can provide the kind of perspectives students may need to understand about the profound implications of family experiences. Moreover, they may enable students to appreciate more fully the family issues that relate to their own day-to-day practice and, indeed, life. They can offer options as to how to face these issues. Movies offer different lenses on how to view the variety of family roles, functions, and so on. Viewing them may pinpoint some core issues affecting families—conflict, intimacy, power.

In a more purposeful and positive way, movies can also help students take a journey across generations, sort out connections, and give a sense of belonging, continuity, and identity. While the movies suggested here may not precisely fit your classroom situation or focus, examining them may suggest ways for you to include movies in your courses.

Babe Though on the surface a film about a pig raised by a dog, *Babe* raises questions for students about their own or clients' families. A poignant portrayal of an adoptee, I use it when teaching a module in the family course dealing with atypical and alternative family styles. It leads to lively and intensive discussion about such questions as: Is it possible to be raised successfully by someone other than your mother? What effect does labeling and stereotyping have (Babe being "definitely stupid")? How did Babe deal with it? Does that give you some ideas for yourself? Your clients? What is the impact of settling for "the way things are"? What can Babe teach you? About staying in one's proper place? What are "cruel victories"? What is nature and what is nurture? Can you stretch past your nature? Can you outgrow your family? What is the importance of crossing chasms? Must we be resigned to destiny? What is the impact of secrets?

Ordinary People A remarkably moving film, *Ordinary People* produces penetrating observations and compelling personal musings. Especially because the class assignments stress intensive examination of students' own family of origin, questions posed often elicit strong feelings—sometimes tears, sometimes silence. Most of these questions are framed in personal terms. What makes a family ordinary? Was yours? Does their pain in any way reflect your own, your clients'? Was your own family out of balance in any way that resembles this one? What do you know about being a scapegoat? Are feelings in your own family shared with one another? Are there secrets you knew existed but didn't quite know exactly what they were? Are there secrets you suspect influence the dynamics of clients' families? With what impact? Was the emotional atmosphere in *Ordinary People* anything like that you grew up with? Does it depict the atmosphere of your clients' homes? How is it the same? How is it different? What does this movie show you about communication difficulties and possible ways of handling them?

Lorenzo's Oil   Based on a true story of one couple's struggle to keep their child alive, this very emotionally gripping movie stuns students and raises for them questions about marital relationships, stepfamily relationships, and sacrifice. Despite all professional and personal advice to the contrary, this couple forges a path that saves their child from death. Are there circumstances in your own family that are recalled by *Lorenzo's Oil*? How did you and your family handle them? If you reflect back on them, how would you handle them the same or differently now? Are there such circumstances in your life now? In your clients'? What would have kept you going despite all odds?

Movies in a Course on Teaching

In a one-semester course designed for doctoral students interested in understanding and enhancing their knowledge, but particularly their skills in teaching, movies play a central role. The course examines the philosophy of education but concentrates on the processes and pragmatics of learning and teaching in both the classroom and internship. It emphasizes examining and evaluating the commonalities and differences among an array of teaching models, frameworks, practices, and strategies.

There are a number of movies about teaching, from *Blackboard Jungle* to *Facing the Music*, from *Small Wonders* to *Lean on Me*. In *Les Choristes* the teacher who is initially derided by unmanageable students ultimately gains their respect and admiration. Taken aback by the school's tyrannical rules and punishment, he takes a detour and introduces the rowdy students to music. In the *Emperor's Club*, a prep school teacher (Kevin Kline) dramatically and compellingly demonstrates the true marriage of method and content by wearing a toga and having his students do likewise. Most of these movies have a common motif—encouraging students to make their lives extraordinary. They accomplish this through a multilayer process that relies largely on the development of relationship and active self-disclosure. Sometimes this works out well; sometimes it is a disaster.

These movies are required viewing before two classes scheduled to focus on evaluation of teaching effectiveness. Having already viewed the movies, in class, students examine in depth a few excerpts selected to demonstrate core elements of the teaching process. They concentrate on the style of the teacher and the impact that differing styles have on the delivery of content and on maintaining the interest of students. They then formulate ideas about ways to evaluate the impact of teaching style.

As an opening exercise to a full discussion of the films, students are asked to visualize a positive teaching experience at any phase of their education. Having this image in mind, followed by viewing a relevant excerpt from a chosen movie, they form into small groups. Their task is to identify, compare, and contrast the characteristics of teachers they visualized with those depicted in the film. A set of questions guide their deliberations: Is there a match between the substance being taught and the manner it is delivered? What is the effect of self-disclosure on students? What is the posture of the teacher? After sharing individual views, student/practitioners collaborate as a group on selecting three common attributes that they perceive as core. They report their findings back to the class. Repeatedly, over time, the predominant themes students identify are:

- Guiding and directing students toward their own learning, as in *Mr. Holland's Opus* and *To Sir with Love*
- Sharing one's own wisdom and experience, as in *The Prime of Ms. Jean Brodie*
- Changing students' view of the world, as in *Dead Poets Society*
- Applying theory in a practical way, as in *The Emperor's Club*

And common to all the films are:

- Developing critical thinking, curiosity, and inquiry
- Imparting information and understanding phenomena
- Challenging existing modes of thinking and processing
- Encouraging discourse and controversy

The Prime of Miss Jean Brodie In Maggie Smith's textured portrayal of the avant garde teacher at an exclusive girl's school, Miss Jean exhorts her girls to follow their hearts and never lose their individualism. But in her iconoclastic shoot-from-the-hip approach at rousing her pupils from lethargy, she oversteps her boundaries by praising the attributes of Mussolini, and moreso, by baring the details of her sex life. Although Miss Jean Brodie displays many of the effective ideas presented in this book—use of media, self-disclosure, relationship building, and so on—she fails, devastatingly, because her methods run amok through self-absorption, disregard for the students, and inappropriate overdoing it. She strays from the main content and merely serves her own purposes. What was the effect of her personal sharing? Did she bridge media and course content? What happens when biases are imposed? Where is the line between the refreshingly unconventional and the pointlessly bizarre? Are unorthodox methods defensible?

To Sir with Love   Though trained as an engineer, teacher Mark Thackeray (Sidney Poitier) sets aside the textbooks and reaches out to his students as mature adults. Obstacles for Thackeray to overcome are the amorous advances of a student, the machinations of a class bully, and the hostility of his fellow teachers. Students report that they respond to Poitier, who, although rather traditional and perhaps even stiff, relates his lesson to real life, while circulating among the students, connecting with them in a genuine way. They see him as not only effectively able to manage the class and the classroom disruptions, but to influence and motivate them, impelling them toward increased learning. Students wonder: Is it possible to be hard-nosed and caring at the same time? What are effective ways to manage disruption in a class? Is it appropriate to disclose personal information? How does culture influence teaching approaches? How does a teacher monitor and restrain strong personal negative reactions? What is the hallmark of fairness?

Dead Poets Society.   The rallying cry of teacher John Keating (Robin Williams) to his students is a memorable *carpe diem* ("seize the day"). Education for most of them is the same old stuff, but Keating takes an unconventional road, ripping pages out of textbooks and asking his students to mount their desks to view the world from a new perspective. While students rarely see themselves as being able to be so flamboyant, they admire that he starts where the students are and shows that humor and creativity does not compromise the seriousness of the lesson. They marvel at his journey outside the boundary of the classroom, which they know many teachers view as sacrosanct. Students actively discuss: How do you assess where the students are starting from? Can one be innovative without being censored? What is the cost of integrity? Can I dare to go outside the confines of the classroom? Is it okay to single out particular students preferentially? Are there boundaries for novelty and creativity in the classroom?

Mr. Holland's Opus   Glenn Holland (Richard Dreyfuss) is a musician and composer who takes a teaching job to pay the rent, while in his spare time he can strive to achieve his true goal—to compose one memorable piece of music to leave his mark on the world. As Holland discovers, "Life is what happens to you while you're busy making other plans." As the years unfold, the joy of sharing his contagious passion for music with his students becomes his new definition of success. Mr. Holland discovers through trial and error that teaching is a most rewarding experience when it draws out the students. He listens attentively to their unique talents and needs. He underscores the notion that teaching and learning can actually be fun. What students most like about Mr. Holland is the way he shows the benefit of individual attention to a student and the learning fostered by his coaching. Questions of students revolve around: How long does it take to be comfortable with the role? How effectively can the separation be made between one's personal and professional life? Is teaching enough? How does one integrate passion for a subject with occupational requirements? How does one define success?

Movies in a Clinical Practice

The stated intention of a required, one-semester practice course is to enhance students' analyses of their practice through written and oral presentation of their own case material. Its focus is refinement of intervention skills. It aims to assist students to integrate knowledge gained in the classroom with their field experience. Students prepare and present cases from their internships with special attention to their purposeful use of self as a clinician. Students are expected to demonstrate their ability to grapple with treatment issues, to show evidence of critical thinking in their written and oral work. Evidence of self-awareness and professional use of self constitute primary focal points. The principal locus of attention is on the relationship between the student and the client. Issues of self-disclosure, transference, and counter-transference invariably arise.

While professionally produced, standard client tapes are included along with demonstration recordings of prominent practitioners from a variety of perspectives—notably cognitive, behavioral, gestalt, and analytic—students most intensely relate to films. Three films, namely *Equus, Good Will Hunting*, and *Don Juan DeMarco* offer sharp and incisive scenes on the class's core themes.

Equus Psychiatrist Martin Dysart (Richard Burton) investigates the unusual violent blinding of six horses by a seventeen-year-old stable boy, the only son of an opinionated but inwardly timid father and a genteel, religious mother. Students are riveted, and some repulsed by action in the movie, but are enthralled by the depiction of a therapeutic encounter. Dysart seeks to unravel all the darkness beneath the youth's savage act. Students are struck by the depth and intensity of the relationship between the psychiatrist and patient, in which multiple transferences are revealed, a basis of the class. As Dysart exposes the truths behind the boy's demons, he finds himself face to face with his own. Students are attuned to another principle of the course, that is, healing for the therapist and the client is equally shared. Students thrash out such issues as: Does the process of self-reflection ever end? What are the ways to make an effective separation when your own and clients' issues intersect? Can therapy destroy creativity?

Good Will Hunting   A janitor at MIT, Will Hunting (Matt Damon) is a disaffected and disenfranchised genius, in trouble with the law, who has a gift for math. Eventually forced into counseling after a series of mishaps, his counselor, played by Robin Williams, helps Will, severely abused as a child, to turn his life around, come to terms with the blows in his life, recognize that there is more to himself than he believes, and realize that what has gone wrong in his life is not his fault. Unlike Burton, who depicts a traditional psychoanalytically oriented, neutral therapist, Williams is self-disclosing, directive, and confrontational—one who is successful in effecting a transformation in both the client and himself. Students applaud his openness, genuineness, and honesty, but have serious questions about his so unabashedly disclosing so much of himself and not fully getting his life together. They often query: Is it possible to be a mess oneself and still be able to help others? Does therapy really make a difference? How do we deal with ending a relationship with a client we really like and may never see again?

Don Juan DeMarco   Don Juan (Johnny Depp), a young man searching for his lost love, feels like he has nothing to live for. He attempts suicide. Dr. Mickler (Marlon Brando), tries to help Don Juan figure himself out and accept his true identity. Mickler, in the midst of his own struggles, comes to believe that the young man actually is Don Juan. He ponders whether Don Juan, having his own reality, is crazy. Through the storytelling of his past, Don Juan instills Dr. Mickler with a new fire for life and love. Students find it interesting to contemplate the challenge in the film that parallels some of their own practice, that is, distinguishing reality from fantasy and breaking into denial. As with *Equus* and *Good Will Hunting*, the issues of transference and countertransference prevail and compel attention as does the notion of the balance between healing and being healed. Is it possible to change another person without being changed oneself? How do we deal with seriously delusional clients? Is it okay to feel "good" about being effective?

STUDENTS' OWN MOVIES

An assignment in another clinical course requires students to interview therapists. In preparing a final assignment, they are expected to create a manual of a particular intervention strategy—cognitive, RET, psychoanalytic, or other—which includes an interview of a practitioner who subscribes to that theoretical orientation. Very often, accompanying the manual is an audiotape, and sometimes a videotape of the interview. One student's film stands out. With permission, it shows her interview with a prominent writer, practitioner, and proponent of the RET approach as she participated in a weekly open forum. Presenting a case of a suicidal client with whom she was preoccupied, she interacted with him as he enjoined her to face the way she unwittingly interposed her own background, sense of mission, and "savior complex" onto the client. She needed to take stock of and rein in her own "stuff," as he named it, and direct her attention to the client and the principles inherent in the RET method. Multiple advantages accrue from students viewing this tape, used with permission. They applaud her courage in embarking on this venture, show appreciation for her making it available to them, acquire an expanded perspective into the theory, witness firsthand the founder of a theory in actuality implementing it, and are induced to follow suit.

GUIDELINES FOR EMPLOYING MOVIES

Dos

Do use movies because they have a unique message to deliver, present content better than another method, and genuinely reinforce the learning objectives. Ask yourself these questions before requiring students to view them: Why this movie/specific episode in particular? What theme is best presented? What does it state or convey better than any other method might? Does it lend itself to creative use—for example, role play, brainstorming, and so on.

Don'ts

Don't use movies simply because they are available, as a substitute for other methods, as a source for entertainment only, as a time-filler, or as a substitute for the immediacy of interactive experience.

SUGGESTIONS

- Assign movies early in advance
- Have them on reserve in the library
- Provide questions before students view them
- Combine them with other methods
- Build in transition or segues to other content
- Role play selected situations

If a movie has certain weaknesses or foci that detract from the main point of the lesson, advance these at the outset and ask students to lay these aside and concentrate on the pivotal parts or messages.

Storytelling

Stories are reminders of how complex, ironic, ambiguous, and fateful life can be. People bring us their stories. They hope they tell them well enough so we understand the truth of their lives. They hope we know how to interpret their lives correctly. We have to remember it is their story.

—ROBERT COLES

Stories are the inspired fields of our brains. Elie Wiesel once commented, "God made man because He loves stories." The outstanding virtue of stories is that they are archetypical in nature and inspire, when shared, a relational partnership in teaching and in learning.

Relish the story! Humans have been referred to as storytelling machines. Why? Because of our profound hunger for narrative. It is instinctive. And because, even when delivered in plain language, stories are crammed full of undercurrents and subtle nuances. Our lives are filled and revealed in stories. Their allure resides in their transcendent quality—transcending person, place, culture, ideologies, and academic disciplines. Although cousins of case studies, critical incidents, and role playing, stories are a fresh and unique breed. They draw us out, lead us beyond ourselves and our immediate situation in special ways. Stories rise above a totally logical and straightforward approach to learning and shuttle back and forth between facts and feelings. They echo Schon's (1983) assertion that stories trigger reflection in a context that presents material differently.

We think in terms of stories. New events and experiences are cast in stories that are linked to previously understood stories and experiences. Knowing them, finding them, reflecting on and reconsidering them—massaging them, as it were—help students to understand and operate in the world of professional practice. Students easily apprehend their meaning and adapt them to their own purposes, eventually capturing or inventing their own. Our ability to tell stories in novel ways is a hallmark of wisdom, maturity, and careful judgment. Stories from our own practice, from students, even from folklore, movies, and mythology can be usefully employed to build motivation in learning environments.

Verisimilitude is the stuff of stories. They cannot be reduced to facts. Stories tell so much more. Words turn into pictures, providing a kaleidoscope of human nature—the ordinary and the extraordinary—about fallibility, about changing the human condition.

WHY STORIES?

Stories are a triumph of ordinary and extraordinary humanity and fallibility. What is a story? Bruner (1996) deems a story as a mode of thinking, a means of organizing experience and knowledge. For him a story is "the way we explain the world to ourselves" and "the way we explain ourselves to ourselves."

Stories grip us in their thrall. And they're simply easy listening, to boot!

We live by telling stories. One of the first things children say when they talk is, "Tell me a story." Stories help us understand who we are and where we come from. They unravel the strands of our existence. Whether quirky, poignant, sad, hilarious, or self-deprecating, stories are one of the world's oldest teaching tools. Mesmeric, they remain engraved on students' memories. Diane Setterfield comments, "A good story is always more dazzling than a broken piece of truth" (2007).

Storytelling is probably as old as spoken language. Certainly, it existed years before written language came into existence and has continued through the centuries when only the few knew how to read. From the beginning of time, people have told stories. They have been the unwritten syllabus of education. Storytelling is an oral art form preserving and transmitting ideas, images, motives, and emotions with which everyone can identify. Storytelling takes place when one person wants to communicate what they have learned from experience with another who wants to listen.

In expert hands, stories take us prisoner. Inventive storytellers capture our hearts, invigorate our minds, and rouse our spirits.

Don't tell your stories merely for the sake of them, as a substitute for other forms of instruction, just to fill time, or just as a detour. Make them integral to your lesson. Storytelling is so much more than a simple rhetorical device. It is a mode of knowing, a persuasive means to appeal to the head and the heart at the same time. It captures the richness and indeterminacy of experience and helps pass on the art of teaching. Stories arouse empathy and provoke thought. Stories facilitate grasping a principle and applying it with originality and insight.

The rationale for teaching with stories is simple. Rather than employing more conventional means, such as lecturing or exploring conceptual structures, students' imaginations are awakened by the telling and unraveling of a story. Stories deliver a cognitive package in intriguing ways. Facts and figures pour in; underlying meanings are indelibly recorded on the brain. Vibrant and touching, stories illuminate practice. A well-told story can tie up previously bewildering factors into a meaningful and understandable whole, as it provides an efficient and rapport-building mode of communication.

THE POWER OF STORYTELLING

The point of storytelling is to preserve the sense of continuity in the web of experience. Our link is through a process of discovery, through human stories that require preservation. This chapter focuses on narrative and storytelling because they are especially appropriate and compelling for adult learners. They provide a method for articulating the self and constructing professional identity. Learning in this venue constructs and reconstructs personal, professional, and social identity. As narrated, stories foster interpersonal relationships and stimulate reflection, frequently leading to a change in their thrust.

Stories are an illuminating way of presenting the complexity and wonder of the human experience in an emotionally satisfying way. They offer a deeper sense of meaning for self and world. They link past with future. They entertain, comfort, explain, and warm. They are healing. Stories also clarify, enrich, ennoble, and stimulate change. Stories embody the human quest for meaning and the universality of finding a way to that meaning. In listening to stories, there is no demand to do, but rather a sharing of a sojourn on life's road.

Capturing the underlying essence of clients' lives counts for so much more than a mere collection of facts and figures, no matter how detailed. Students recognize the profundity inherent in them and, for example, in reading vignettes. In *Elements of the Helping Process: A Guide for Clinicians* (Fox, 2001), student/practitioners are stirred to spontaneously and eloquently tell their own. They are particularly moved by "Sylvia's Story," as well as by the stories of four traumatized, suicidal men. Their avid and enthusiastic reaction to these stories paves the path for their recounting their own lives. Extemporaneously, students report their having overcome the challenges of eating disorders, addictions, mental and physical disabilities, and surviving traumatic events. These commentaries penetrate the very core of professional practice, making all who listen better attuned to the tribulations of clients and more appreciative of getting past facts and seizing underlying complexities.

Our own stories as teacher/practitioners, as well as those of students', are often compelling and consequential.

Stories celebrate the ordinary events of daily life. They explain the extraordinary occurrences of life. They capture the natural and supernatural. They transmit culture, values, religion, and history. Stories prepare children for adulthood and are told over and over again for the purpose of teaching the lessons of life. For adults these life lessons are given a current and universal context, a new place in an earlier remembrance. And they entertain.

Stories are all around us. Draw upon them as teaching tools. They encourage students to see the world through the lens of the storyteller. They increase students' receptiveness and pleasure in learning. Through storytelling, students learn to utilize storytelling themselves as a way to elicit and fathom clients' history, pursuits, aspirations, strengths, abilities, deep-seated needs, and wants.

Stories present ideas in ways compatible with students' natural thought and conversational processes. Certainly more fascinating than such mainstream methods as lecture, stories, stored and organized narratively, make retrieval easier and more complete. Stories themselves are meaning-making. When sharing stories, new meanings emerge that strain against and challenge conventions. They counter-balance dry and sterile texts and flat and tedious lectures.

THE APPEAL OF STORIES IN THE CLASSROOM

Storytelling creates a climate of mutuality. Teachers as well as students invariably bring stories into the classroom. As storytellers share wisdom and experience, listeners share reactions and are enticed to contribute their own. All learn from the experience because stories are intensified through the very interchange between tellers and listeners.

You assume the role of co-collaborators with students during the exploration of meaning in stories. You model for them a method of inquiry and mentor a style of learning. Stories reinforce the notion that learning is an active, exciting process.

Storytelling brings heightened awareness to the teller and to the listener—a sense of wonder, mystery, and reverence. The sharing of experience creates communion in the strictest sense. Your willingness to be vulnerable, to expose openly your values and beliefs, creates rapport.

A central appeal of stories as teaching tools is their ability to appeal to students with different styles of learning. They evoke both right-and left-brain responsiveness. The teller's cognitive message is enhanced by its evocation of mood and affect. On the basis of brain research, we know that a story resembles the way the brain works. Its weakest function is the retention of isolated data bits. The brain does not hold onto bits, but it does grasp and hold onto wholes. Stories tap into the mind's recesses. Deduced (left brain) while visualized (right brain), stories improve retention as well as recall. Hearing a story, the right hemisphere plays a special role in decoding visual information, maintaining an integrated structure, appreciating humor and emotional content, deriving meaning from past associations, and understanding metaphor. At the same time, the left hemisphere plays a special role in understanding syntax, translating words into their representations, and deriving meaning from complex relations among word concepts.

Students get the gist of the story, its meaning, its message, more clearly and readily than from some other methods of instruction. Busy envisaging the tale as words are told, these pictures have staying power and are integrated into students' memory. Images remaining in the mind form associations. Students tap into these associations and continue to process their messages and themes long after the story is told. They retrieve pictures of the action, the characters, the story line. These pictures integrate and access memory. Remembered long after orations, stories serve almost as mnemonic devices to recall lessons. Students connect new knowledge with stories and lived experience, weaving them into their own narrative of meaning.

SOURCES OF STORIES

A particularly vibrant source of stories is your own practice and teaching experience. Students respond to genuine illustrations from your own practice that either illuminate conceptual content or expose your flops and hits. They find them intriguing.

Another source of stories is film. Stories from the movies are striking in their ability to generate students' commentary about human emotions—love and hate, loyalty and treachery, hope and despair.

Literature is nothing but stories, oftentimes magnificent, poignant, compelling stories. *The Little Prince* is required reading for a doctoral course, the Philosophy of Science. At first glance, students find it to be an unusual, indeed strange, choice in a doctoral program. Yet, dissecting it in a unit devoted to measurement, they grasp its intent: Can all things be measured? What distinguishes quantitative from qualitative research? Is there only one true scientific approach? Does the heart know what the head can't? Are methods derived from the physical sciences appropriate in the social sciences? In this same course, students are required to read a novel, *The Alienist*, in addition to texts by Thomas Kuhn, Karl Popper, and other philosophers of science. This story captures, in a distinctive way, the course's major questions addressing strongly held preconceptions about science—objectivity, subjectivity, value-free-ness, bias control—as well as the influence of politics, culture, religion, power, and gender.

On a similar note, students in clinical courses, many of whom have themselves undergone counseling or therapy, consider the novel *August* to be on target in terms of the effect of countertransference and the result of practitioners' absence. The Harry Potter series, a modern fairy tale also available as movies, buttresses and enlivens discussion about such crucial yet dry topics as ethical dilemmas.

Children's stories such as *The Little Engine That Could*, and *Oh, the Places You'll Go* to highlight how they can be utilized in work with children. These taut, deceptively simple stories do more than entertain; they instruct on an impressive scale. Their simplicity, as is the case with most stories, belies their profundity.

Myth, folklore, and fairy tales—from Persephone of Greek myth to Jack of beanstalk fame—provide inventive ways of looking at recognizable client dilemmas, quandaries, tests, as well as quests. Students comment that these stories are enlightening metaphors for them as well. Stories allow us to remember what happened in them, freeing us from having to learn their lessons the hard way in real life.

Stand back somewhat from your own discipline, connect with other disciplines to locate stories. How refreshing it is for students to have you dip into their interests—current movies, music, fiction, art—to capture their attention and propel a lesson forward. At the same time, you model ways for them to assimilate popular culture into their work with clients to propel it forward.

In sum, stories connect students to each other and to you while proposing innovative ways to effect change. Their value lies in arousing students' interest and in exposing everyone to different interpretations, moral lessons, and frames of reference.

MASTER STORYTELLERS

Lewis Carroll called stories "love gifts." They embody universal themes and offer new windows on the world. They explain what might otherwise be unexplainable.

Stories have been the mainstay of master teachers and practitioners. Jung (1954) spoke of stories, folk tales, and myths, and their meaning in human experience. Joseph Campbell (1988) described four types of stories: the mystical, the cosmological, the sociological, and the pedagogic. Mystical stories are sources of awe, inspiration, and comfort. Explaining the universe and human existence, they form the basis of theological and spiritual exploration. Cosmological stories, predating science and written history, ordered and explained the shape of the universe. Sociological stories transmit culture and values. Pedagogic stories, "teaching tales," guide the way life is lived. They inform our inner lives and instruct us about harmonizing our lives with reality. All stories speak to our common as well as our unique journeys.

Joan Laird (1989) sees stories as descriptions of life transitions and inner and outer transitions. To be asked to tell a story is empowering. For her, in asking for a story, complexity can be presented without the demand to do anything about it.

Clarissa Estes (1992) sees stories as connecting people to alternatives and possibilities. They encourage change, enliven relationships, repair hurts. She believes that stories offer a road map for change. For her, stories are lessons and guides that can set one's inner life in motion and open doors that were previously closed. Since storytelling is much older than the art and science of therapy, Estes sees storytelling as "joining humanity across time and space" (p. 73). Her approach involves finding the right story at the right time.

Bruno Bettelheim (1976) describes how stories and fairy tales illuminate inner problems as they externalize internal issues. They arouse curiosity and present a frame of reference. Stories enrich and stimulate feelings and thoughts and encourage finding one's own solutions. Most important, stories and fairy tales offer hope; while adversity permeates them, the struggle to get through them pays off. The value of the stories is hearing the students' interpretations, for there will be different meanings, moral lessons, and frames of reference to be considered.

Coles (1989) uses stories to prick students' consciences and increase their awareness of the moral quandary caring for people often puts them in. Stories are reminders of how complex, ironic, ambiguous, and fateful life can be. They help understand the truth of people's lives. Coles believes that stories are instructive for the teller as well as the listener. Telling the story changes the teller when he or she is able to connect to the immediacy of the human experience. Hearing the story changes the listeners when they are able to enter others' lives. Stories comfort, refresh, feed the soul, and display our common humanity. Stories highlight conflicting values and incongruities in the human condition.

Stories can be new or old, edited or spontaneous, structured or rambling, improvised or rehearsed. They can report the ordinary—those things we take for granted, that we are hardly conscious of at all—or the unusual. Through stories you collaborate with students to uncover fundamentals of human behavior and professional helping. Stories reinforce the notion that learning, as practice—as, indeed, life—is a dynamic, active, exciting, and creative process.

CHARACTERISTICS OF STORYTELLING

Successful stories do not follow a prescribed framework; they are not formulaic. They nevertheless seem to include a clearly defined and believable message or theme, are vivid and somewhat dramatic yet can be simple and brief.

Successful stories are contextualized and are compatible with the course and class focus. They are realistic and close to the listeners; cover familiar territory; have a beginning, middle and end; and do not ramble on and on.

Unlike scientific discourse, wherein thinking moves deductively from the general to the particular, stories move thinking inductively from the particular to the general. In addition, they appeal to feelings, in contrast to the logical ways we have been taught to process information and to learn. As Blaise Pascal observed, "The heart has its reasons, which reason does not know."

Do not tell stories just for the sake of telling stories, as filler, or as self-aggrandizement. Be careful not to allow them to distract from the lesson's main emphasis. Stories, no matter how poignant, need to be woven into the web of course goals, content, and theory.

YOUR OWN PERSONAL AND PROFESSIONAL STORIES

Peek into a typical practice classroom while a lecture is in progress. The teacher may intercede from time to time in order to emphasize an important piece of information, perhaps even taking the time to point out a significant theoretician. The faraway looks on many faces of students convey disengagement, boredom. After what seems like an eternity, you notice a stirring; students appear all too anxious to leave. Rising from their seats with a sigh of relief, they are thankful that the class is over for another day.

Down the hallway, a similar lesson is being offered. In this instance, students are rapt. Their focus is clear, they are wide awake. The day's topic is similar to the former class, but the format is different. It is more casual, interactive, engaging.

It differs considerably from the conventional textbook/lecture method, which typically offers a brief and usually bone-dry synopsis. Storytelling captures attention and conveys material. Narrative trumps exposition.

Teachers have a deep and rich repertoire of personal, practice-based, and teacher-based stories and experiences to share with students. These stories are frequently of considerable pertinence to the situations that students deal with. They allow students to appreciate that similar circumstances, unanticipated moments, problems, and dilemmas have occurred before, and there are productive and instructive ways to deal with them. Most often they signal success. Mine your stories for their metaphorical punch, not for the sake of reverie or nostalgia.

Each of us develops a unique interpretation of content and of teaching episodes. These interpretations, which continue to be reshaped by experience, are woven into coherent narratives. Some years ago, however, I saw them as non-scholarly. One day a student spoke to me after class.

This student said that he wished that I did not quote so many well-known experts in the field. He believed that he and many of the other students would much rather hear about my practice, my feelings, my insights. They would rather get to know me and the way I interacted with clients than to hear about more famous thinkers. Somewhat taken aback and embarrassed by his remarks, I was grateful to him. He was on target. It was just another time when I was hiding behind a mask of intellectuality. It was so much easier to quote someone else than to speak from my own experience and from my own heart. It also isolated me from students' immediate experience since it kept me from getting close to them and them from getting close to me.

Because listeners tend to co-construct stories, students, hearing your stories fill in the picture, imagining what it was like. In other words, they weave the tacit and well as explicit point of the stories into their own fabric. Hearing your stories, students become acquainted with your knowledge and skill. They reflect: Are you open or closed? How do you guide them? Can you laugh at yourself? Are you able to see things differently, imaginatively? Can you reform and revise your opinions? Do you take your own advice? On this note, Do you evince with them through your stories what you expect them to evince with clients?

Stories from your own experience rise above specific details to overarching patterns and themes relevant to professional practice. Beyond face value, they foreshadow for students what they might face themselves down the road.

The subtle interface of art and science in practice is so difficult to express in words. This exquisite balance is the hallmark of clinical practice. It is equally difficult to capture in straightforward terms the inspired intersection of the humane and the technical. Broaching the topic through a personal story succeeded in doing exactly that.

A few years ago, unsuspectingly and without symptoms, through a routine checkup, a tumor was detected in my head. After immediate but inconclusive medical tests—MRI, CT scan, blood—it was determined that rapid intervention was required. Consulting with three renowned head and brain surgeons at leading teaching hospitals led to the conclusion that it was inoperable. One doctor, after conducting a biopsy through the roof of my mouth without anesthesia, stated, "Nothing can be done." Another two specialists pronounced that the best thing to do was to go home and update my will. No determination could be made about malignancy. All concurred that it was a rapidly growing and dangerous intrusion.

Having heard the name of one esteemed doctor from a number of sources, I contacted him. Away at a conference giving a workshop, he would not return for a few days. Begging for an appointment upon his return, I saw him five days later. Hearing first what other doctors recommended, and before studying the medical test results, he proceeded with a physical examination from toe to head. He commented, "Images and records are far less preferable than contact with a patient before advancing an opinion. I do not operate on scans, I operate on people." He continually explained what he was doing and why.

Gently touching me and using warmed instruments, he gave a reason for every move he made. Toward the end of the examination, displaying the scans on the light screen, he pointed to the tumor's suspected cause—a runaway molar. Observing that it was truly unique, that he had never seen one before, he nevertheless expressed certainty that it could be excised. He pointed out the multiple risks of surgery, including possible severing of the fifth nerve on the face, but explained as well as the risks of not having surgery—going deaf and blind within a short time. As it happened, my daughter was due to graduate from college that weekend. I mentioned this as he phoned to schedule an operating room. Without diminishing its urgency, he scheduled the surgery for three days later.

The doctor informed me that there was no certainty as to whether the tumor was benign or malignant. At the preparation he mentioned that upon awakening after the surgery—if my face was bandaged, the tumor was malignant. If not, it was benign.

Since this was an unusual surgery, the case was on grand rounds throughout an eight-day stay in the hospital. Awakening, there was no bandage. It was benign! But I couldn't see. As residents, interns, nurses, and oral surgeons stood at the bedside, the doctor commented, "You can't see." Whereupon, putting his hand lightly on my knee he gently said, "I'll fix that." Getting up, he went himself to the window, adjusted the blind, returned to the bed, and said, "Now you can see." Indeed, I had been staring directly into the setting sun.

He didn't delegate a mundane task to assistants. He undertook each step along the way, no matter how great or small, himself, with expert precision and human kindness. What an amazing and elegant blend of art with science. This man was a paragon of technical competence and empathic care.

No further explanation is required. *The cornerstone of healing is human connection.*

STORIES AS EMPOWERING

Stories connect you, the subject you teach, the students, and the student's practice situations. Real-life stories lead to an empowering recognition that storytellers are at once main characters, narrators, and authors. Stories, as real-life people and situations, can change.

Novice clinicians, but especially novice teachers, may suppose that true professionals—real veterans such as yourself—do not feel. That is, they rarely experience disappointment, uncertainty, frustration, confusion—they have moved beyond emotional reactions and face issues of practice and teaching with utter rationality and dispassion. It is both instructive and beneficial, however, for beginners to hear your stories, which not only serve to dispel these beliefs, but show that you are, above all, human. You react to setbacks. You are affected by them. But you face them squarely and endeavor to surmount them. Thoughtful accounts of problems and those of exhilaration set a realistic stage. There have been numerous times when teachers have had to scrap what they were doing and start over again. Earlier chapters chronicle some of the many times failure had to be acknowledged and students were invited to critique the approach. Collaborating earnestly with them helped design new ways to proceed.

Master teachers approach each new semester based on evaluative feedback from previous classes. They comprehend that this fresh group of students has a character different from former ones, that their learning styles and goals are perhaps at variance with former ones. Do not take for granted that you can teach the way you previously taught, even with identical course content. Yes, it's anxiety-producing to continually start anew. It is also exciting. Keep in mind the revitalizing, humorous, sometimes triumphant moments of past classes.

STUDENTS' STORIES

At the beginning of courses, ask students to tell a story of how they got into the class. Typically their tales are superficial—by subway, by car, by accident (because the class fit into their schedule). Latecomers complain about highway jam-ups, train delays. Less commonly students tell gripping sagas— dramatic career shifts, a mentor's advice to obtain credentials for themselves. Students at times come from backgrounds resembling those of their clients— backgrounds full of adversity, defeat, and sadness, but also of hope and triumph. These inspiring stories lead naturally to a consideration of course goals.

In one instance a student opened up with this story:

> My dad was in prison. My mother was on crack. We were a family of ten, not all of us by the same parents, and my older sister, fourteen, ran the household, living in the projects. Basically bringing ourselves up, my mother was in rehab, out of rehab; home, not home. When home, often high. She'd be around for a while and then disappear again for months.
>
> We ended up in foster care with all of us in different homes. My foster mother used me as a slave to do all kinds of dirty house work. She could barely remember my name. She had three children of her own and three other foster kids. I started not eating. I went to four different foster homes and ended up in a treatment facility. I ran away but came to see that people who had money, weren't in jail, didn't take drugs, or get killed all got an education. A counselor in school took an interest in me even

though I had a bad attitude. She got me into college. She didn't give up on me. I ended up graduating with honors from a city college. Long story short: here I am going for my master's degree.

Allow students to reveal material in a way that is natural and comfortable. It makes interaction human and pleasant and furthers engagement in knowledge and skill-seeking. It can also have drawbacks and get the class off track. Approach stories such as this one with respect and be sure to relate it quickly and unequivocally to the course. It was not offered gratuitously, but in a class based on the practice and policy of adoption and foster care.

Storytelling crystallizes students' personal, cultural, and professional identities.

On another note, enlist students in the telling of their stories through diverse assignments. A family treatment course, for example, carries the expectation that students trace their own family of origin by creating a storyline. Two preliminary written assignments precede their composing a story about their family. The first involves conducting a study of their ethnic backgrounds from an intensive study of the literature explaining the characteristics, traits, and culture of their heritage. How well does your family of origin "fit" this picture? How does it differ? How does your background affect you? What do you subscribe to or reject? How does it influence your practice of "professional helping"? The second assignment calls for them to develop a three-generational genogram describing the family patterns, conflicts, relationships, and unique features. Students are asked to evaluate its influence on their becoming a therapist. After these two hefty assignments, they compose a story about their family, citing stories told to them—red letter days, achievements, skeletons, emigration, and so forth. They venture hypotheses, invent yarns, and render plots that are evocative and emotionally charged.

Not necessarily a typical final paper, students fashion remarkable formats for these stories. Elaborate albums are fabricated, including photographs, mementos, postcards, and certificates of baptism and marriage. One video stands out, depicting a family's history back to the *Mayflower*.

All persuasive stories are composed of a setting, characters, props, a plot, and a narrative line structured into a unitary whole. Recounting them, we transmit more than just facts, often enthralling and riveting accounts. Implicit in the thoughtful rendering of stories are revealed central motifs—personal growth, mishaps, particular problems, dilemmas, coming to terms with ideology, finding outlets for frustrations, discovering new direction, gaining insight into previously unknown parts of self. Stories invite rapt attention. Restructured through reflection, they stamp an indelible mark on memory.

Case/Critical Incident

Teaching carries an awesome responsibility to encourage students to want to know, to show them how to know, and to insist they ask, for what purpose do I need to know?

—C. R. CHRISTANSEN

The core of teaching is the serious obligation to "touch" students. Providing more than the mere rudiments of knowledge is essential. Involvement is critical. Case study and critical incident examination are means to that end.

To become competent practitioners, students need to develop the ability to incorporate knowledge, and, more important, to apply it in their practice. At the end of the day, student/practitioners will have clients in front of them for whom they need to decide what action to take.

Prerequisite know-how and skill involve understanding clients' motivation, background, thinking, behavior, affects, and concerns, combined with external forces affecting their lives. It includes the disciplined ability to select strategies and techniques appropriate to clients' conditions and circumstances. Lead by example. Students pick up what they observe you do. Just as you endeavor to provide a rationale for what you do with students, so students gather how to provide a rationale for what they do with clients. Disciplined practice demands that practitioners continually monitor and evaluate their efforts to assure consonance with professional values and ethics. The case method encompasses all of these facets.

Before entering the workforce to face flesh-and-bone clients, the case method provides students with an impressionistic chunk of reality. They become stakeholders in credible dilemmas. While certainly not perfect recreations of true situations, case studies, compared to other methods, bring students closer to what they need to keep in mind when dealing with real people.

The case can *be* the lesson.

As mentioned throughout this book, a parallel exists between what happens in the classroom and what happens in clinical practice. Cases—particularly in the manner in which you draw upon them interactively—exemplifies for students how they might deal with similar client situations. To use it to its best advantage, consider that the very manner you respond and interact with students as you ponder cases demonstrates for them ways to respond and interact with clients.

THE CASE METHOD

The case method is predicated on three key notions of instruction. The first is that creating an open environment and selecting active methods that value students' contributions enhances learning. Second, when you are personally relevant and available, and students are more fully engaged with the learning materials, a synergistic effect emerges. Third, knowledge, built upon prior life experience, brings learning close to the reality of practice. At the same time, it builds from the tangible to the conceptual. Case study is simultaneously enjoyable, engaging, and edifying.

Cases move away from any bias toward fact-feeding lectures to meet the challenge of situation-specificity. Rather than emphasizing theory formulation, cases tailored to course objectives with imaginative narratives become theoretically relevant and vibrant. The complexity of the human condition is such that each case offers a unique study unto itself. Teacher/practitioners guide students to induce from case material an appreciation of theoretical patterns and skills applicable in novel practice situations.

Case studies rely on the premise that knowledge-building is continuous and incremental. As scaled-down replications or simulations of real-life experiences, they are designed to contain ample information to generate independent reflection and person-to-person connecting. Cases confront students with situations resembling those they may face themselves day to day. Relying on a high degree of identification, cases assist students to explore their own attitudes and examine their own conduct, as if by analogy.

When, with sensitivity and flexibility, you draw out students' reflections on case material, lessons come alive. More important, students master reflexivity. Discussing what goes awry and what goes well, students are challenged to explore, explain, and evaluate practice in light of underlying theories, assumptions, and values embedded in the cases. Opportunity is provided for them to appraise professional judgment, skill competence, and conditions that influence the need to explore alternative or new ways of thinking.

A further advantage of case simulation is that it exposes students—who might otherwise be unfamiliar with different cultures, customs, and traditions—to a diversity of client characteristics. Examining someone else's case from a protected and detached third-person vantage point also reduces defensiveness and paves the way to frank consideration of alternative viewpoints and interpretations.

As mentioned throughout this book, practitioners do not learn from the book. This is especially true because they function in indeterminate zones, that is, areas involving value conflict and uncertainty. They must rely on discretion and improvisation, constantly "inventing and testing in the situation strategies" of their devising (Schon, 1987, p. 5). Through selective use of case material, combined with the processes of modeling, mentoring, and mirroring, you prepare students for taking stock of their attitudes, biases, shortcomings, attributes, and skills for undertaking work in these indeterminate zones. Cases are faithful to Dewey's philosophy "not to teach truths but to teach men to think in the presence of new situations" (Dewey, 1974).

What happens in the classroom, therefore, while not identical, resembles what happens in the practitioner's office. Your interaction with students related to case material reflects the kind of critical thinking, skill competence, and professional judgment expected of students in their work sites. It depends on conditions you create to encourage "freedom to learn by doing in a setting relatively low in risk, with access to coaches who initiate students into the 'traditions of the calling' and help them, by 'the right kind of telling,' to see on their own behalf and in their own way what they need most to see" (Schon, 1987, p. 17). In other words, the artistry of good teaching involves learning by doing in a way that allows students to reflect on their perceptions, connect theory to work with clients, articulate abstract ideas, and adeptly handle complicated and unforeseen situations.

MERITS OF CASE STUDIES

Clinical practice is replete with challenges necessarily involving complex legal, dynamic, administrative, and ethical dilemmas. It calls for preparing students to tackle difficult problems through hands-on experiences rather than lectures filled with principles and procedures. Experiential measures create problem-solvers who can define issues clearly, adjust to change easily, develop autonomous skills, and compare possible solutions readily rather than merely retain or recite facts and figures.

An added advantage of case method is that it is adaptable, that is, it can be orchestrated to reach students with different learning styles. For example, the sensor, a literal learner, responds to the sense of reality provided by the real-life scenarios and believable characters in cases. The intuitor is inspired by the opportunity to creatively develop and offer ideas and fresh solutions to the problems depicted in the case. Thinkers respond to the logical elements of the case and pay close attention to details. Feelers balance thinkers by emphasizing the case's affective components.

The diagram shown in figure 3 represents the process students undergo as they tackle a case situation. The case method initiates and maintains discussion, deliberation, and, at times, fruitful debate. In doing so, it fosters a higher level of cognitive skill as well as its affective accompaniment. It stretches students' thinking beyond habitual molds and boosts their emotional resonance. It requires students to provide evidence supporting their positions. It enhances retention, recall, and application of knowledge into actual practice settings. Most significant, it spurs thoughtful inquiry, rigorous analysis, and systematic reflection and self-appraisal. A special benefit of the case method is that students move beyond being passive absorbers.

Mnemonic devices serve a variety of purposes. For students, they establish associations with information to be learned, which, in turn, evokes a mental image for the learner. They thereby can spur the learner's memory to recall desired information. They enable students to recall material because they offer an easy means to remember what was said. They permit you to speak to the subject matter without continual reference to notes, which can be distracting for both you and students. They enable elaboration on various relevant points without losing momentum or sacrificing the main point. In this instance, the merits of the case method can be abbreviated as four Cs: *complex*—it has no ready or unitary answers; *critical*—it presents situations from many perspectives; *comprehensive*—it evokes a big picture; and *creative*—it offers novel and innovative viewpoints.

Working interactively and collaboratively, engaged in invigorated discussion, students become co-learners and co-teachers as they deal constructively with their colleagues. The give and take of ideas, opinions, and frameworks provides exercise in transmitting one's own ideas and attending to those of others. Listening to competing and controversial views offers new ways of examining material. Generating evidence to support positions hones students' knack for justifying their stance and supporting their proposed courses of action. Students come to recognize that cases, as real-life events, exist on a continuum, that few problems have pat solutions. In this regard, the case method promotes pooled insight.

DEVELOPING CASES

Towle (1954) speaks in detail about the selection and arrangement of case material. She advises teachers not to select cases exceeding students' levels of development. Towle's is a developmental continuum that runs throughout the students' educational experience, developing and building upon analytical skill each step of the way. She emphasizes the need for continuity and

Figure 3. Tackling a Case

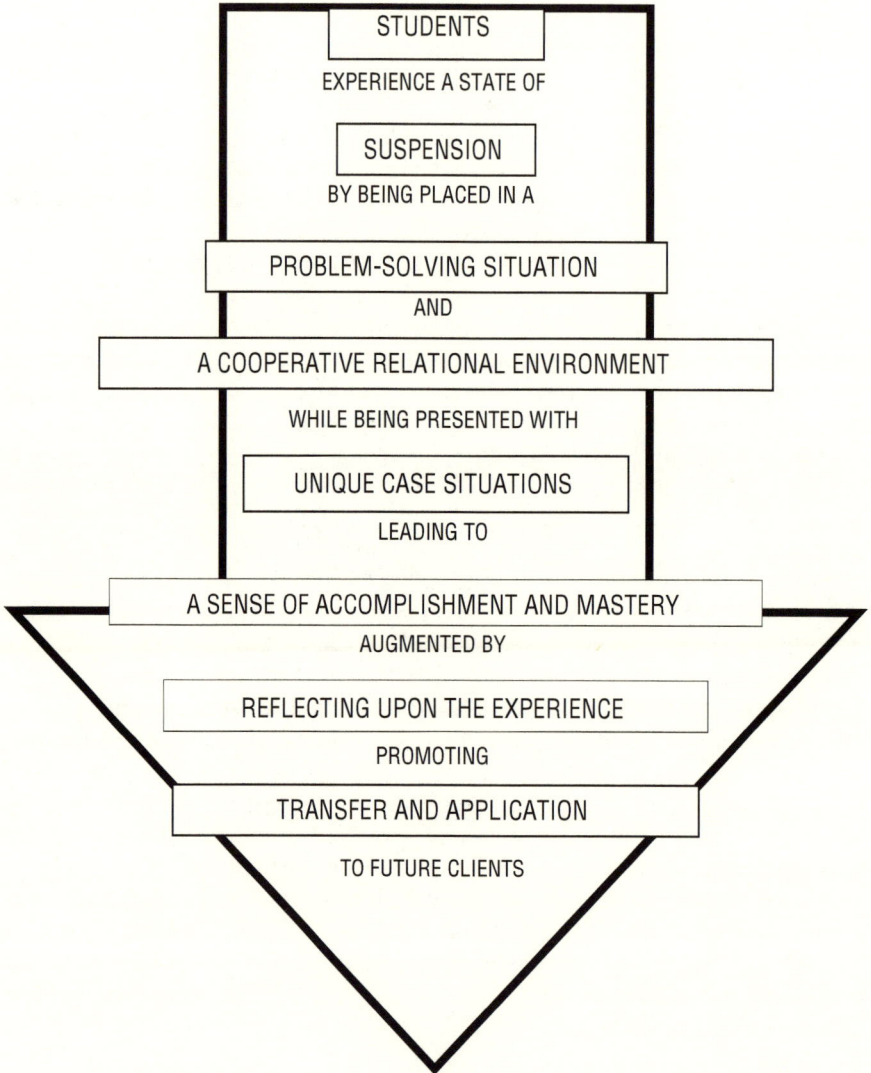

STUDENTS

EXPERIENCE A STATE OF

SUSPENSION

BY BEING PLACED IN A

PROBLEM-SOLVING SITUATION

AND

A COOPERATIVE RELATIONAL ENVIRONMENT

WHILE BEING PRESENTED WITH

UNIQUE CASE SITUATIONS

LEADING TO

A SENSE OF ACCOMPLISHMENT AND MASTERY

AUGMENTED BY

REFLECTING UPON THE EXPERIENCE

PROMOTING

TRANSFER AND APPLICATION

TO FUTURE CLIENTS

sequencing of experiences as well as case material always attempting to teach the parts in relation to the whole. She recommends selecting cases only as far as they fulfill particular learning objectives and considering them in pairs so as to highlight comparison. Attending to Towle's advice, choose narratives that fulfill the particular learning objectives for the course, whatever their source.

Again, a mnemonic device, the five Cs of well-developed cases are: *concrete*—they simulate issues from everyday practice; *clear*—they are germane to course content; *contextual*—they highlight environmental influences; *challenging*—they challenge stereotypes and preset ideas; and *catalytic*—they inspire interaction and dialogue.

Keep in mind that your primary attention needs to be directed toward your students; therefore, in selecting the right case for the right moment, do not be arbitrary, rather, draw upon your intimate firsthand understanding of your group of students, their learning styles, stage of development, and former responses.

Whether presented in writing or orally, recognize that it is impossible to tell a whole story in one succinct vignette. Select essential details and omit those that make little difference in the overall picture for apprehending the crux of the case.

Provide ample background information sufficient for students to get the gist. Cases challenge you to sketch a meaningful situation that reflects complexity without over-focusing on specifics, being mindful of the details that could inextricably alter a seemingly simple problem. In your selection, censor as much as possible your own personal attitudes, predispositions, and biases about a real or a hypothetical situation. In this way, students tackling the case are not led to conclusions you may tacitly or inadvertently convey. Embed the scenario with current issues, concepts, and dilemmas to serve as a springboard for constructive examination. Consider concluding the case with the lessons it manifests.

Customize the case rather than provide "armchair" cases that apply anywhere and, as a result, nowhere. Develop scenarios that approximate as closely as possible the type of circumstances students presently face or will encounter in the future. Make them as naturalistic and realistic as possible. They will spice up the class.

SOURCES FOR CASES

Students' Brief Reporting

In reviewing students' reports or journals, you may find an excerpt that exemplifies a concept or skill that is the focus of attention in the syllabus at the moment. It may also happen that a student raises a question or an issue about a client spontaneously in class providing an immediate and authentic sample of that focus. Make the most of these since they provide insights rarely described in texts.

Following is one sentence from a student's lengthy case record that became a stimulus for class deliberation about theory: "Ms. V has not followed the medication protocol prescribed by her psychopharmacologist for generalized anxiety."

This single sentence led to exploration in light of three theories that had been the focus of attention to that date—behavioral, psychosocial, and cognitive. The class was divided into three groups, representing the three respective theories. Over the course of ten to fifteen minutes, each group applied specific content from their reading and lecture in the analysis and solution to the issue of non-compliance. At the end of the small-group working time, the whole class reconvened for reporting. Each group took five to ten minutes to report on their perspective.

The group assigned to the behavioral model, for example, analyzed the case from this perspective and developed a plan using that model to work out a viable response to the problem. Each group in turn similarly reported.

As each group presented its analysis, other members of the class critiqued and deliberated about the group's analysis and solution. Try to reserve your own commentary to information that may be inaccurate, in error, or unfounded, or to provide additional data, stimulate hypotheses or reactions, or respond to questions the small group itself could not clarify.

Seemingly simple and uncomplicated at first, Ms. V's single-sentence case evolved through group discussion and evaluation into a complex and multifaceted situation with an array of interpretations and a variety of strategies for solution.

Working in this way from case material in whatever format provides opportunity for your class to identify problems, analyze the components of the problems, and devise appropriate solutions. You can choose to reinforce learning by making explicit connections between the case and students' work settings. It is possible to expand such a scenario further. It can consume a portion of a class, an entire class period, or be spread out over several classes by gradually adding increasingly complex data as sketched out later in the chapter.

Cases are multifunctional, offering a range of possibilities for intensive examination—articulating the dynamics of a situation, generating courses of action, evaluating the strengths and weaknesses of courses of action, generalizing from a conglomerate of symptoms, refining diagnoses, or assessing the efficacy of intervention. You can also emphasize precipitating factors or stressors, resources and strengths, and pertinent attitudes and stereotypes.

Students' Formal Presentations

Students' more formal case presentations can occur either spontaneously or selectively as previously described. They tend to follow a prescribed format. Following are sample instructions for composing a case presentation for a clinical sequence capstone seminar.

Case Presentation

I.   One week before your class presentation, distribute to all members a case summary following the outline provided, a sample process recording, and a selected annotated bibliography related to the case.

II. Your presentation should be more than a recitation. Refer to, but do not read, your notes. Involve the class in discussion.

III. For your final paper, write a three- to four-page reflection on your semester's work, which includes a subjective exploration of your research, your presentation, and your learning during this seminar. Include an explanation of how your experience during the case presentation and subsequent discussion altered or enriched your understanding of yourself, your clients, your work, and/or your profession.

Below is a guide for outlining a case presentation. When there is a wide range of diverse students with a wide range of case populations and a wide range of problems, such a structured format provides a uniform pattern for presentation, systematic analysis and discussion.

Case Outline

I.   Brief description of client(s): identifying data
     A.   Strengths, skills, abilities
     B.   Unique features
     C.   Cultural, spiritual factors, etc.
     D.   *DSM* diagnosis

II. Brief summary of clients' history and background
     A.   Family constellation (genogram)
     B.   Brief summary of clients' issues, problems, etc.

III. Brief assessment of clients' functioning
     A.   Target issues; auxiliary issues
     B.   Capacity and motivation
     C.   Themes, patterns, style
     D.   Barriers to improvement and progress

IV. Outline of the contract
     A.   Treatment goals
     B.   Time frames
     C.   Evaluation procedures

V. Impressions
    A. The quality of the relationship
    B. Special observations about the clients
    C. Evidence of treatment progress
VI. Specific issues
    A. In working with these clients
    B. In better understanding yourself
    C. In applying theory
VII. Questions for class discussion

Your Own Case Material

Early in the semester for a module dedicated to beginnings, this abbreviated and edited version of an intern's first interview at a local outpatient veterans' hospital with a diagnosed paranoid schizophrenic man returning from an overseas inpatient facility is introduced.

10/16: The purpose of this first interview with Mr. G was to acquaint him with the treatment program and initiate a relationship.

Mr. G was one-half hour early. He is tall, well-groomed, very serious, and intense. He spoke slowly in a precise manner.

We spoke about literature after I had noticed and mentioned that he was carrying a book by Ralph Ellison. I learned that Mr. G does much reading and concentrates on what he referred to as "naturalistic, realistic" writers like Dostoyevsky, Gogol, Turgenev. He said that he prefers "black modern" writers because they say things that "mean more" to him. He does read nonfiction.

He majored in English literature for two years at a prestigious college and thoroughly enjoyed it. He wanted to be a teacher but, as his studies progressed, he began to withdraw into himself, becoming unable to concentrate and function. As a result, he dropped out of school, which was a crushing blow to him. He "clammed up." I mentioned that I had studied English at one time and that perhaps our mutual interest might help us understand and deal with his problems and gradually open up his shell. Mr. G silently considered this for some time and then reported that he knew what I meant and was willing to try.

Talking about what he does with his time, Mr. G said that he walks through Harlem. He mentioned how different things are from the last time he had been home from the service.

After a long silence, Mr. G asked when I would see him. As I started to write out the appointment card, I mentioned that I would try to get the Ellison book he was reading so that we could discuss it. Mr. G offered his hand to shake and left.

The class is divided into four groups. Each group acts as a panel of experts in supervisory consultation about the contact. In the time provided, they discuss and assess this case in terms of the effectiveness of this initial interview, including: the exchange in terms of focus; what went wrong, what went right, and why; did the client return?—why or why not? These "panels of experts" then recommend what to do differently if it were to be done over again.

Often, students' feedback is highly critical about the fumbling, rampant intellectualization, avoidance of emotional content, leading of the client, and a host of other mistakes they had just been warned about in the textbook. There is also recognition of the positive connection made, that is, "meeting the client where he currently is," a principle recommended in that text. Almost always, students make sound observations and recommendations for improving the interview.

Beyond the benefit of collaborative figuring out a real-life case, additional learning accrues. After the students' critique, I admit that this is my own first case record. Ideas are generated as to why I share this faulty record with them. Invariably students comment that the messages flowing from this review and conversation are meaningful, hopeful, and helpful. Among these messages are: it is possible to move eventually from being an inept, inexperienced, and floundering intern to another level of expertise; the internal process of self-examination and reflection hones knowledge and skill, leading to self-correction; the external processes of consultation and training, but principally supervision, contribute to becoming a more experienced and capable practitioner.

Professional growth is incremental, continual, and achievable.

Cases from Training Manuals

The Sanchez case is drawn from a training manual prepared as part of a teaching casebook, *Generalist Social Work Practice with Individuals, Families, and Groups* (Ravazzin Center, 2003). It demonstrates the potentials inherent in the case method combined with feasible approaches to working with the aging.

THE SANCHEZ FAMILY

Mr. and Mrs. Sanchez, aged seventy-seven and sixty-eight, respectively, have been raising their two grandchildren for the past five years. Maria (age ten) and Tony (thirteen) were orphaned five years ago when their parents (the Sanchezes' daughter and her husband) were killed in an automobile accident. The children's father was driving home with his wife from a party where he had been drinking heavily. Neither of the Sanchezes' two other children were in a position to take on parenting responsibilities. Mr. Sanchez is retired from a position with the post office. Mrs.

Sanchez supplemented their income by cleaning apartments. Approximately two months ago, Mr. Sanchez suffered a stroke, which left him with considerable impairment. He has been admitted to a rehab facility, where he is progressing well, and the expectation is that he will be returning home. He currently has some speech impairment and is partially paralyzed on one side. It is not clear how fully he will recover, but the expectation is that there will be some residual impairment. It is not clear how he will be able to manage as the home has two stories, and the only bathroom is on the second floor.

Prior to Mr. Sanchez's stroke, Tony was beginning to get into trouble at school. This took the form of sassing his teachers and failing to do his homework assignments. Last week, Tony assaulted another student and was therefore temporarily suspended from school. Maria, always a quiet child, has presented no problems at school, although her teachers have noticed that she now spends more time by herself.

Mrs. Sanchez initially was able to handle things with the same determination and task-oriented focus that she used to deal with the loss of her daughter and her transition to the parent role for her grandchildren. However, Tony's suspension from school has taxed her beyond her ability to cope. Mrs. Sanchez has become weepy, unable to focus, and unable to make decisions. She has had difficulty explaining to Tony and Maria what is happening to their grandfather. She has not told Mr. Sanchez about Tony's suspension.

Mrs. Sanchez is called to attend a meeting with the school principal and social worker. When the social worker asks Mrs. Sanchez if she could give them any insight into why Tony has become so aggressive, she bursts into tears.

A framework is also suggested for operationalizing the case:

A. Identify the precipitating factor(s) that brought the family to the attention of the social worker and principal
B. Identify the presenting problem or problems
  1. Tony and Maria's behavior
  2. Mr. Sanchez's physical condition
  3. Mrs. Sanchez's psychological functioning (stressed)
  4. Adequacy of home environment (to accommodate Mr. Sanchez's physical needs)
C. Identify the client
  1. Mrs. Sanchez?
  2. The Sanchez family?
  3. Tony? Maria?

D. Identify current stressors
1. Role transitions (multiple) for Mrs. Sanchez and Mr. Sanchez
2. Delayed grief reactions (for all members of family)
3. Loss (job, physical health, stroke, death of parents and children)
4. Goodness of fit with environment is disrupted by stroke and Tony's suspension from school
5. Environment (house with only bathroom on second floor)
E. Identify the resources within the individual, family, and community
1. Mrs. Sanchez—resilient but seems very depleted
2. Apparent lack of informal support (extended family)
3. Questionable formal supports (social security, pension, Medicaid for the children)
4. Identify the legal status of grandparents caring for children
5. Identify school supports
6. Identify missing information about social supports, such as the Sanchezes' two adult children, friendships, religious affiliation
7. Identify and know how to inquire about coping style, that is, the strengths that have enabled the family, especially Mrs. Sanchez, to handle previous stressors
F. Identify attitudes and stereotypes toward aging and older adults

Cases from Textbooks

As with most texts dealing with clinical practice, my own book, *Elements of the Helping Process: A Guide for Clinicians* (Fox, 2001), contains numerous case studies alluded to in classes. When addressing them, however, aspects of the cases not covered in the text itself are emphasized. Students, having read the material in advance are prepared to actively react to alternative ways of approaching the material. For example, one chapter titled, "Who Says I Can't?" unveils the story of Sylvia, who survived multiple childhood physical and sexual traumas, became quadriplegic as a result of a skiing accident, and eventually earned a reputation as a celebrated artist. This case, when discussed in class, raises all kinds of questions not extensively addressed in the text about resiliency, stamina, nature versus nurture, life's ironies, and transcendence over seemingly insurmountable odds. These topics become the locus of attention.

Developing a Spontaneous Composite Case

A particularly noteworthy procedure for probing a case that engages all members of the class is extemporaneously developing one on the spot. It usually emerges from the immediate need for a tangible example of a complicated concept under study that students are just not getting. Each member of the class at large is asked, in turn, off the top of their heads, to offer any random fragment of information. It is then recorded on the board. Contributions continue until a sufficient amount of data is noted to create a composite picture. Students, divided into small groups then organize and categorize the information into various dimensions, again outlined on the board—for example, identifying information, diagnoses, explicit and implicit observations, impressions. This exercise of spontaneously evolving a case scenario at first seems contrived. Students, in creating the case, assume a degree of ownership for it since it includes material they have contributed. They therefore become more actively involved in analyzing it. Over the years students have remarked that this type of seemingly haphazard, make-believe case is remarkable. It aptly captures and reflects aspects of situations that absorb them at their internships. It helps them face trepidation and address unpredictable and challenging issues.

SELECTING CASES

While cases emerge from textbooks, training manuals, journals, movies, plays, and anecdotal retrospective reports from you and students, they can also emerge from other more up-to-date sources, such as newspaper reports, television exposés, white papers, letters, diaries, or archival information. Clearly, the origin of cases is varied and multifaceted.

Whichever type of case you select, be sure to adequately prepare for its assessment. Give careful forethought to avoid stumbling through. Be sure to consider how the case intersects or mingles with other conceptual, theoretical, and evidence-based foci. Fashion it as a narrative, and not just a bundle of information.

Again, a mnemonic, five Cs of case relevance. Cases should be: *compelling, concise, current, and crafted* to encourage discussion and dissent; finally, *characters* should be believable.

Be certain that the cases accurately reflect real-world situations and succumb neither to over-simplification, over-dramatization, nor over-generalization. Endeavor to have them as closely as possible parallel students' experiences in the field.

A major decision faces you. What is the intent of the case? Can you afford a range of interpretations? Is it meant to offer a sample problem that elicits reactions, solutions, thoughts? Does it mine unique or universal characteristics? Does it represent singular and specific or generic qualities? Or is it meant as an exemplar of professional practice portraying how an expert might intervene? What do you hope to have it accomplish?

PRESENTING CASES

Presentation is most often incremental. Begin the semester with less complex cases and move to more complicated and multilayered ones as the term advances. Each class then adds new layers of approach and knowledge. This layering is found as well by the students as they see clients. Each class brings new information, new insights into clients, new dimensions, and previously unmentioned problems to be considered and analyzed.

Consider yet another incremental method—using one case throughout the semester, gradually adding over time new data, new issues, new layers each week to mimic real life and real clinical practice in all their complexities. Each successive reading or reconsideration eventuates in refined examination and critical analysis.

On the other hand, a series of different cases may be nested together for purposes of comparison or counterpoint. Again, these may consume one part of a class or an entire class.

Whether you have students peruse cases in advance in textbooks, handouts, library, or e-reserve, start the class by reading the case aloud. It freshens recollection and may spark additional thoughts. Provide careful directions—orally, written, graphic—for review of cases.

Guideline questions are crucial. Submit them to students in advance. Make sure that the questions relate specifically to the purpose and focus of the lesson at hand. For example: What issues are denoted? What diagnosis fits? What is the best plan for intervention? What would happen if . . . ? What are the options? What theories relate to the case? What values are in evidence? If you were the practitioner, what would you do differently, the same? What are the positive and negative aspects of the practitioner's work? What might be the difference between how a novice and an expert might handle the situation? What is your assessment of outcome? How does the case resemble your own workload? Such questions sharpen students' awareness of themselves, their clients, their skills, and the extent of their knowledge, along with their learning progress.

The case method has disadvantages: not providing a total recreation of the situation, the result of its analysis not being implemented and evaluated, its being slow, its possibly leading to over-generalization. Yet its advantages—when employed purposefully and with discrimination—far outweigh its disadvantages. Case study can lead to or be combined with other constructive methods—role play, writing, debate, brainstorming, storytelling. Conclude case discussion with a method that focuses on its applicability and transferability to internships.

THE CRITICAL INCIDENT PROCESS

Critical incidents resemble, but are different from, cases. They are more specifically focused on events that are surprising, unusual, worrying, and/or compelling in their immediacy. While cases tend to be retrospective in nature, the potency in critical incidents arises from their currency. Typically "war stories," they present an opportunity to reflect *in* and *on* action (Schon, 1983, 1987). Underpinning the critical incident approach is the belief that thinking and feeling and attitudes will change during a reflective process about behaviors examined in light of a critical incident. They interface formal education with what students face in their daily work.

Especially convincing and captivating for students are the ways you deal with critical incidents, teachable moments, seizing the moment, or, as Jane Addams referred to them, "moments of perplexity." They comprise enlightening "turning points" as lessons unfold. Through them you can demonstrate in class how to tackle atypical spontaneous occurrences.

Moments that do not fit the prescribed curriculum are outside the ordinary and predictable. Artistic and intuitive processes are required. Introducing on-the-spot experiments, like the one described earlier in the chapter, with subsequent explanatory commentary, students witness firsthand within the classroom the flair of an expert practitioner. They are not necessarily as dramatic as those referred to in other chapters of the book. For example, a student in a clinical class, while reviewing a case involving an incarcerated domestic abuser, described her gut disgust at this behavior. She spurted out that she was herself an incest survivor. Acknowledging and honoring her subjective reactions, without exposing them openly in class, led to a review of ways that might be employed ordinarily to attend to such phenomena and avenues for help, and offered additional resources to peruse.

In another instance, a student began crying as she discussed the termination process in therapy. Grieving for her own recently deceased father, she was able to identify her feelings, recover her composure, and explain what dynamics of loss she experienced. In this situation, because her sharing did not violate an unresolved private and anguishing predicament, reiterating her comments as characteristic of termination was adequate. These unprompted critical incidents can be incorporated or adapted for transfer to their transactions with clients. They epitomize what Schon (1983) refers to as applying new discoveries, which, in turn, lead to new reflection, spiraling "through stages of appreciation, action, and re-appreciation (Schon, 1983, p. 132).

In such exchanges you, as an on-site practitioner, provide students with continual feedback about your process. It demands a willingness to be vulnerable since it requires that students and you expose internal thinking and feeling to each other. Taking advantage of particular occurrences requires awareness, sensitivity, openness, and flexibility. There are few better ways of engaging students and demonstrating the relevance of self-examination to their personal and professional lives.

Students need to learn to be conscious and disciplined in their relying on discretion and improvisation, constantly "inventing and testing in the situation strategies" of their devising (Schon, 1987, p. 5). So too, you, through modeling, prepare students for such an undertaking. It fits closely the paradigm for experiential learning advocated by Kolb (1984).

Critical incident reporting entails students identifying a specific charged event with as much specificity as possible. The description should follow the incident as close in time as possible to remain current and viable. An outline for capturing such an event resembles fairly closely the outline presented earlier for process recording. The difference here, however, is the attempt to avoid or forego too-hasty speculation, interpretation, or analysis. Rather, the emphasis is on remaining true to the factional occurrence, providing a faithful rendering of the event. It includes relevant details and circumstances surrounding the event, the people, and the role that students play. After describing the incident in detail, ideas are advanced as to why the incident was critical, what stood out, what were concerns at the time, what was learned. Consideration is directed to what went particularly well or poorly, what were some mistakes or missteps, what was especially demanding and challenging.

A doctoral class in teaching epitomizes a method for critical incident appraisal. As a condition of being a teaching assistant (TA), students are required to write about the crucial episodes, patterns of response, and the interdependence between the teaching process and real life as they experience them in their teaching. These incidents are a core mechanism of communication between you and students, students and fellow colleagues, students and their own students. Their review helps direct focus and refine lessons. Reports of these critical incidents, shared as an integral segment of each class meeting, become reliable means for monitoring thoughts, actions, and feelings when they are fresh in students' minds. They are a running account of the chronology of the changes that occur during the teaching process. These narratives are not stuffy or static descriptions but, rather, dynamic unfoldings which reveal how students draw upon their understanding to make meaningful connections, make decisions, and solve problems.

Grasping, distilling, and making explicit the activity that is salient in the here and now of the classroom experience enables students to understand that both the teacher and student capitalized on the material presented in class to create a real learning moment for all involved.

Photography, Art, and Quasi-art

Not only is there an art in knowing a thing, but also a certain art in teaching it.

—CICERO

Photographs and artwork celebrate and evoke creativity and curiosity. Stirring a thirst in students for delving beyond words into deeper consciousness, planting kernels of curiosity, whetting their appetite for learning counts for much more than pouring information into their heads.

Photographs and artwork play a prominent part in my teaching and practice. While I have absolutely no talent in either art or photography, each nevertheless has educational and therapeutic value in sharpening students' cognitive ability and honing their emotional sensitivity. It is frustrating to convey the elusive essence of photography and artwork as educational adjuncts. They have a palpable impact on learning, practice, and fostering productive and healthy interaction. Both photography and art embody so much more than words can say. They offer for teachers and students alike a more raw and honest means of communication than words do. They change ways of seeing.

More than for their aesthetic impact, photographs and artwork are versatile and riveting in teaching. They nurture spontaneity, reduce distance between students and students, and students and you. In the long run, images have staying power. They remain in students' minds far better and far longer than words do. They promote retention and recall. They help to make the invisible visible by compressing intangible and ephemeral ideas into concrete form. They transform the intangible and tacit into the graphic and tangible.

Photographs and artwork, drawn upon in a variety of ways, amplify key points, direct attention to non-traditional material, arouse an array of senses, and appeal to different learning styles. Because they are so palpable, the language of visual line, color, and image deepens comprehension. Photographs

140

and artwork readily trigger associations. No question, "A picture is worth a thousand words."

Words sometimes have a tendency to obscure meaning. Have at hand a diversity of nonverbal techniques for student expression. A multidimensional approach makes it more possible to access the inner person.

Photographs and artwork make it possible to go beyond talking; they speak a language of sensation and symbolization. The distinctive benefits of using photographs and artwork are stimulation and motivation, definition and elucidation. This chapter focuses on the dos for the selection and development of these techniques, presents examples from actual teaching situations, and offers guidelines for their use in the classroom. Capitalized on in class, they become auxiliary methods for students to adopt or adapt in their work with individual, family, or group clients.

PHOTOGRAPHY

Susan Sontag calls photography an ethics of seeing, a medium that almost by accident yields truths it does not intend to tell. The camera does not lie. She highlights the usefulness of photographs, suggesting that they provide a tool for dealing with things everybody knows about but does not admit. They manifest what is not seen. Sontag states, "A photograph passes for incontrovertible proof that a given thing happened. The picture may distort, but there is always a presumption that something exists or did exist, which is like what's in a picture. Whatever the limitations . . . or pretensions . . . a photograph—any photograph seems to have a more innocent, and therefore more accurate relation to visible reality than do other" mechanisms (1977, pp. 5–6). Elsewhere she comments, "Words alter, words add, words subtract," while photographs simply reveal and "have an insuperable power to determine what we recall of events" (2004, p. 25).

Photography adds another dimension to storytelling. It appeals to the right hemisphere of the brain, making it possible to access information about students and present information to them that may not be readily available using traditional verbal methods. When combined with a high degree of interactive involvement, photographs bridge understanding of intricate dynamic patterns and affective subtleties. Jung believed that images in and of themselves have a special power to heal. He recommended accepting them in their own right and with their own power.

Photographs motivate and engage students in a non-threatening way to be expressive rather than explanatory. They build rapport by visually showing a story, invariably stimulating others to share their own story. They invigorate lessons.

PHOTOGRAPHS IN PRACTICE COURSES

One instance of photographic power occurred in an advanced course in individual treatment. John, a thirty-four-year-old clergyman, a former client of mine, firmly believed that he was "over-attached" to his mother from early on in his life. He supposed that he "leaned on her for everything" and was convinced—despite examination and reexamination of this phenomenon—that he repeated this dysfunctional pattern by overreliance on other people for gratification and approbation. Verbal interpretations made no headway in altering his skewed perception of his relationship with his mother. At a loss as to how to proceed, he was asked to bring in any photographs of his mother and himself when he was a youngster. Reluctant at first, even quizzical about the request, John eventually produced a series of pictures. Looking at them together, in picture after picture, a remarkable feature became apparent. Each and every picture showed John's mother leaning heavily on him, literally draped over him, appearing to envelope, perhaps even engulf him. À la Sontag, the photographs furnished evidence of an accurate and genuine—perhaps even grave—image of the earlier state of affairs. John was correct about the symbiotic relation, but not his role in it. Indeed, it was John's mother who overly leaned on John, not the reverse, which he for so long believed to be true. *He* held *her* up, supported her. John recognized from viewing the photographs that his perceptions were skewed, misplaced, erroneous. The corrected perceptions led to a shift in his thinking. The discovery catalyzed further exploration and insight, eventuating in a shift in his current behavior. Students find this example startling. ("You'd actually ask a client to bring in pictures? Isn't that too personal?") They are nevertheless astounded by the impact of viewing photographs. Students are even more astounded when they themselves participate in the process of photographic review in a family therapy course.

PHOTOGRAPHIC GENOGRAM

A course in family therapy concentrates on the students tracing the dynamics of their own family of origin as a requisite starting point for effective intervention. Students are expected to study their own backgrounds through conventional genograms coupled with the extra facet of scanning photographs of their respective families.

Genogram construction is a standard procedure in family therapy. Time is devoted in the course to surveying, developing, and implementing this characteristic tool. Composing a genogram, students graph their family's structure to accumulate data, to track relationships across generations, and, ultimately, to reframe issues. As it unfolds, it documents visually, both literally and figuratively, slices of time and space in the inner workings and meaningful events of their families. The genogram adds to their tool chest of techniques to use with their clients. Photographs, however, as an additional constituent in the process, boost its clout.

Looking at family photographs, albums, scrapbooks, and movie stills provides even more striking idiosyncratic data toward unraveling and understanding families. Emblematic, photographs make visible otherwise elusive affairs, alliances, relationships, schisms, patterns. To demonstrate their impact, a few students are asked to volunteer to bring photographs of their own families to class for us to scrutinize.

Hesitant at first, as are client families, to undertake an unusual and revealing drill displaying their personal memorabilia, students are understandably reserved about exhibiting personal data in the presence of virtual strangers without their identities being disguised. It is as big a step for students to undergo this bona fide process as it is for clients. Nonetheless, they are for the most part agreeable and express appreciation for the know-how that emerges. The act itself of amassing photographs before class resembles what clients undergo in family treatment. Retrieval prompts various reactions and recollections. Collecting and selecting the photos for the class is emotionally charged. They are X-rays of the heart. What pictures are hidden in closets? Which ones are carefully framed? Of whom? Which photos hang on the wall? Which are carried in a wallet? Which are boxed and wrapped? Which are loose and carelessly scattered? Which were passed on from whom? What keepsakes are found among them—dried flowers, memorial cards, postcards, letters, obituaries, birth announcements? Who is taking the photograph? What is the occasion? Does the photographer appear in any photographs? Which child appears with which parent? Who is not in the pictures? Are things seen that were never seen before? Are they tattered or well cared for? Sorting through them alternately arouses elation or angst. It prompts deep contemplation. Jointly viewing these cogent and uncluttered photomontages fosters a bond and creates commonality and community in the class. Setting up a blanket on the floor to establish an identifiable boundary and symbolizing a safe place, volunteers slowly place photographs on it, commenting extemporaneously all the while, with barely any prompting. It makes no difference where they start because the fabric of the family is woven in an ever wider pattern. Gripping stories flow—grandparents' extraordinary acts of courage related to surviving immigration and resettlement hurdles, parents' incredible feats of resilience escaping the Holocaust, ancestors' remarkable achievements facing astonishing bigotry and injustice.

These occurrences emerged from looking over snapshots. There are other forms of photography that can also be creatively utilized in teaching.

Students have creatively drawn upon motion pictures, slides, sepia prints, tin plates, blow-ups, and videotape.

For those who want to preserve a memory, record a special event, or relay a special message, videotape may be the superior, walking, talking alternative to still photos. In another course in family therapy, for example, a mature student entering a second career—unusual in a class of mostly recent graduates—crafted a historical video of his family tree. Enhanced by imagery selected to metaphorically reflect a tree with roots and branches, he incorporated into it a wealth of material: clips from home movies and footage from TV documentaries; still shots of birth, marriage, and death certificates; on-camera interviews with living family members; passages from diaries and notations from a family bible; engravings from books; obituaries from old newspapers; and specially chosen music. The video, which tracked his lineage back in time to the landing of the *Mayflower*, had an almost surreal flavor. Showing this visual treasure to the class and hearing their accolades, he eventually produced the tape for professional distribution, a stunning endeavor. It catapulted him unexpectedly into yet another career path.

Photographs need not only originate from students. Newspapers, magazines, e-zines all provide inspiring images. One colleague uses up-to-date photojournalistic essays in her course. For example, in August 2006, the *New York Times Sunday Magazine* published "Children of the Storm: Where Hurricane Katrina, and We, Have Left the Kids," an article accompanied by eighteen black-and-white photographs. She mounted copies of the photographs on a display board for the class. Students circulated around the room in silence just to observe the photographs. They were asked to note their reactions: What did you observe about the children? What did you observe about the photographs? What reactions did you have to both the children and the photographs? What kinds of questions does it pose for you? Next, the students pretended in a role play to be a team of consultants visiting New Orleans a year or two later to develop a meaningful response to the devastation. Forthcoming from this exercise came a wealth of discussion about post-traumatic stress disorder (PTSD), disaster relief priorities, child protective services, and programmatic deficiencies, all leading to an enriched course focused on child and family welfare. Because of the unprecedented success of this photomontage experience, in a recent faculty meeting, she discussed ways she planned to use photographs from a more recent *New York Times Sunday Magazine* piece titled "Children of God," devoted to an exposition of the young women from the polygamist Fundamentalist Church of Jesus Christ of Latter-day Saints to introduce a unit devoted to attachment theory in the same child and family welfare course she teaches.

To amplify photographs' intense effects, I employ sculpting, a method developed in family therapy. Following genogramming with sculpting compounds students' cognitive understanding of the synchronistic effect of serially building one technique upon another. Students are eager to explore the synergistic effects of amalgamating and building upon multiple intervention techniques.

ART

Art is densely layered. It offers fodder for self-expression and self-discovery. We talk in words but tend to think in images. Take advantage of artwork to convey essential messages rather than struggle to translate them into words. Verbalization, as our primary mode of communication, tends to disguise; art exposes in unexpected bursts.

Art transcends technique, skill, and scientific knowledge. It is one of the most incisive forms of human expression. Figurative and pictorial representatives are better suited than language to tap the way we perceive and process information and form ideas. Images, powerful sources of visualization of persons, objects, or experiences, offer such quality. Imaging can evoke other sensory modalities—sounds, tastes, and smells. When students are asked to imagine, they imagine not only people or places but the feelings that are connected to them. Perception is altered.

Elaborate or fancy equipment is not required to take advantage of working with art in your teaching. A few basic materials—paper, pencils, crayons, magic markers—are all that is needed. Art projects do not call for artistic flair; stick figures, doodles, or squiggles are sufficient. Only infrequently will you meet blind alleys or frustrating responses from either students or clients as long as an artwork task is approached with optimism, encouragement, and support.

Not narrowly conceived of as art, various forms of artwork—diagrams, graphs, tables, illustrations—appear throughout this and other books. Students have referred to these artistic renditions as particularly helpful in illuminating complex material.

In *Elements of the Helping Process: A Guide for Clinicians* (Fox, 2001), for example, a draft of a jigsaw puzzle appears in the form of a sketch of a phrenology head. Students alluded to it as having "staying power" in their recollecting the multiple interdependent factors involved in undertaking a comprehensive client assessment. In this same book, a diagram depicting the dynamics of the life story, in the form of a grid featuring components of past, present, future, conscious, and unconscious elements, further delineated with ovals, although nearly impossible to describe here, makes the life story's stereoscopic nature more plain and decipherable than the academic narrative surrounding it.

A series of sketches of fallen angels by Jane, a former client, exemplify the unspeakable clout of art. Unable adequately to express in words her despair and distress, her "brokenness," Jane's first sketch was a forbidding picture of a morose stone angel statue memorial sunken into the ground. It recalled for her a monument she saw in a cemetery near her home—the same one, she believed, that inspired the title of Thomas Wolfe's masterpiece, *Look Homeward, Angel.*

Over time, as a result of reflection and the time she spent in therapy, her angel softened, her pose shifted. The angel became more fluid, and the time-lapsed form saw it mounted, better, elevated on a pedestal with outstretched arms.

Only minimally able to verbalize her feelings, Jane created drawings that quietly imparted the story—a symbolic metamorphosis from dejection to exuberance. Artwork such as this awakens in students the desire to experiment with artwork for themselves as well as for their clients.

HANDS-ON

Fascinated by the angel sketch, some students venture with their assigned journals in selected courses to "drop color," a method inspired by *The Artful Journal: A Spiritual Quest* (Carey, Fox & Penney, 2002). The combination of tints, inks, paints, and writing adds both a visual and colorful dimension to their words. When blending color with words, new perspectives and insights blossom forth. This enhanced piece of writing harnesses untapped, nascent, yet fertile associations that lead to deep-seated contemplation. Students relish the process as well as the product. It is projective as well as descriptive, a novel and complementary way of journal maintenance. When color is added to words, or words to color, rich and fertile reflections are amplified. Engaging both sides of the brain stimulates awareness and creativity. The right brain, the realm of images, operates holistically, synthetically, and intuitively. The left brain, the realm of words, partializes, analyzes, and reasons. The right brain is more subjective. The left brain is more objective. Journaling that combines images and words enhances each. It is recommended that students occupy themselves with the process. When they get stuck coloring, they write. When they get stuck writing, they color. Shuttling between the two hemispheres is freeing and can return them to the initial method more refreshed.

ART AND SCIENCE

Picasso said it so well: "Art is a lie that helps us to understand the truth or at least such truth as is given for us to understand." Einstein commented, "Imagination is more important than knowledge." These two quotes introduce a doctoral course unit in the Philosophy of Science module, the "relationship between art and science." Its focus—scientific research as well as creative art are set by inspired vision. Both art and science have moved away from the sensory to the realms of the theoretical and abstract in the pursuit of truth. Both are enterprises of discovery, begin with observation, rely on similar forms of metaphor and analogy, go beyond nature, endeavor to rise above the literal, translate data into higher orders of conceptualization, plumb into deeper levels of significance, locate patterns and themes, decipher underlying meaning, and seek general truths. They are complements of one another.

Envelopes containing a series of six randomly shuffled copies of a portrait of a woman by Picasso are distributed to subgroups in the classroom. These were painted in 1886, 1920, 1938, 1941, 1946, and 1962, although students do not know the dates they were executed. Each group's task is to arrange the portraits in order of their evolution and to explain the reason for the particular organization. After the groups collaborate independently, they place their respective portrait set horizontally on a large table in front of the classroom. Usually, the groups follow one pattern, placing the earliest portrait *last*. It is the most representative, realistic, and almost photographic rendering. Students ordinarily arrange some combination of the more modernist, abstract, and cubist renditions first, attributing the depicted evolution to realism as Picasso's finally "having learned how to paint well." The actual chronological order of the portraits is then placed above the other portraits on the table, with the 1886 version appearing *first*. "What's the point?" The point, readily detected by students, relates to the class, the doctoral program, the comprehensive examination, the dissertation, the entire journey of discovery in research and science. All demand less recapitulation of the obvious, less restating of the known, and more elucidation of the obscure, more exposition of the unknown. The nature of the experience shifts from the act of realistic representation. It is replaced by abstracted extraction. In each and every one of the doctoral students' endeavors, rising above the literal, simple, and mundane to the conceptual and complex is crucial. Transcend surface and appearance, seize the big idea, intercept the underlying essence. To synthesize, to generalize beyond concrete experience and specific occurrences, and to reduce and categorize a welter of diverse phenomena into identifiable regularities is the point.

LEARNING FROM A MOBILE

Students sit silently in a family therapy class, watching a crude homespun mobile made of bent hangers and colored construction paper fashioned in different-sized circles and squares circulate in front of them. I comment, "A family is a mobile," and then ask them, "What makes me say that?" Together we figure it out: three-dimensional squares and circles (males and females) of different sizes (adult and child) and colors (individual personalities) circulate around each other with seeming randomness yet having an underlying, perhaps invisible consistent pattern within a circumscribed space: a visual dynamic metaphor of family. In constant motion, changing, and, in so doing, affecting each part in multiple ways. There is seldom a recognizable duplicate configuration. All constituents, however, are inextricably intertwined by strings as they are suspended in balance. A playful art piece, the constellation concretely captures the abstract notion of homeostasis. A viable representation, the mobile's playful quality belies its depth. Variations in configuration, juxtapositions, and shifts in proximity bring home the lesson. Former students claim that the message is hard to forget. It is emblazoned on their memory— family as mobile, a system in constant motion requiring an external force to interrupt its habitual flow to institute change in direction, pattern, structure.

MAPS

The importance of drawing is widely accepted as a clinical tool. It is the basis of a number of psychological tests such as the Draw-a-Person Kinetic Family Drawings and House-Tree-Person Technique. D. W. Winnicott was an early pioneer in using drawing when working with children. He developed the Squiggle Game, in which the therapist and child takes turns elaborating upon an original squiggle and then tell what it looks like (1971). Drawings are used widely as projective means of obtaining information concerning sensitivity, maturity, intelligence, flexibility, and personal integration. Perhaps drawing's major contribution is its linkage to symbolic expression and healing as proposed by Jung.

Mapping comprises an integral segment in a clinical course module focused on the termination stage of treatment. Timed deliberately to coincide with the ending of the course, and indeed, the capstone course in a master's program, it seems an opportune moment to introduce mapping, yet another artistic method to capture the subtleties of ending relationships. Termination concludes a unique interpersonal endeavor. It signals for students, as it does for clients, a unique transitional period. It provokes at the same time a sense of loss and of sadness, but also a powerful and significant experience of growth, a marker of change, of moving on. Mapping symbolically traces students' journey over the semester. Its purpose is to reinforce learning, bring closure to the class, tie up loose ends, provide a means of reflection on learning, take leave, and make a possible transfer to their work with clients. It symbolically illustrates significant accomplishments that are difficult to state in words.

These are bare-boned directions: "Create a map of your experience in class over the past fifteen weeks. Take time to ponder before your draw. Let it stir. Picture the experience and capture it with an image. Occupy yourself with the image, engage yourself playfully with it. Let it flow. Respect it as it emerges. Try not to censor or edit it."

This nonverbal essay is emotionally moving and sometimes draining. Your role in this exercise is not to analyze or interpret but rather to act as a catalyst, a facilitator.

Attend to the process; watch, note, and, where appropriate, encourage the flow of the process. Ask students about their images—details, forms, colors, shapes—not about meaning. Wait until students are ready to explain. The process of discovery is attained by students finding their own breakthroughs in the images they create.

After completion, students, one at a time, voluntarily display and expound upon their maps to the class. Discussing the details and detours of their maps opens avenues to verbal sharing. One variation of the exercise involves the entire class cooperatively creating a collective map.

Like metaphors, maps are less denotative, intellectual, and interpretative (left brain) and more connotative, intuitive, and imaginative (right brain). Following are some prompts for beginning the exercise: "Please tell me about your map." "Does it have a story to go with it?" "Do you detect any noticeable patterns?" "Do these surprise you?" "What do these patterns say about your experience, about what you have learned?" "What steps can you take now to alter any themes that concern you, to enhance those that enlighten you?" "Based on what patterns you have discovered, what would you predict for your future?"

The three map illustrations depicted in figures 4, 5, and 6 are presented without any accompanying statements by the students who drew them.

PICTOGRAMS

While not strictly art, there is an assortment of other pictographic procedures to employ in class to augment learning. These methods tap into essentials that may be inaccessible in any other way. They are particularly useful in small group dynamics seminars rooted in the conception of the class as group. They chart development and growth of the individual students as well as of the class as group with diagrams. One tool, a task-centered projective technique based on the sociogram of a symbolic diagram, actively depicts relationships vividly and concisely. On the board, or better, on newsprint (so it can be saved and resurfaced later for purposes of comparison), draw a large circle. Basic instructions delivered orally sound something like: "This circle symbolically represents the class. The circle creates a boundary around you and the other members of the class." In the first variation, to determine how students perceive themselves in relation to each other and where the group is in its total space, continue with the direction for each student in turn and separately to place a smaller circle representing him or herself within the larger circle. When this task is completed, the next step involves each student

Figure 4

Figure 5

Figure 6

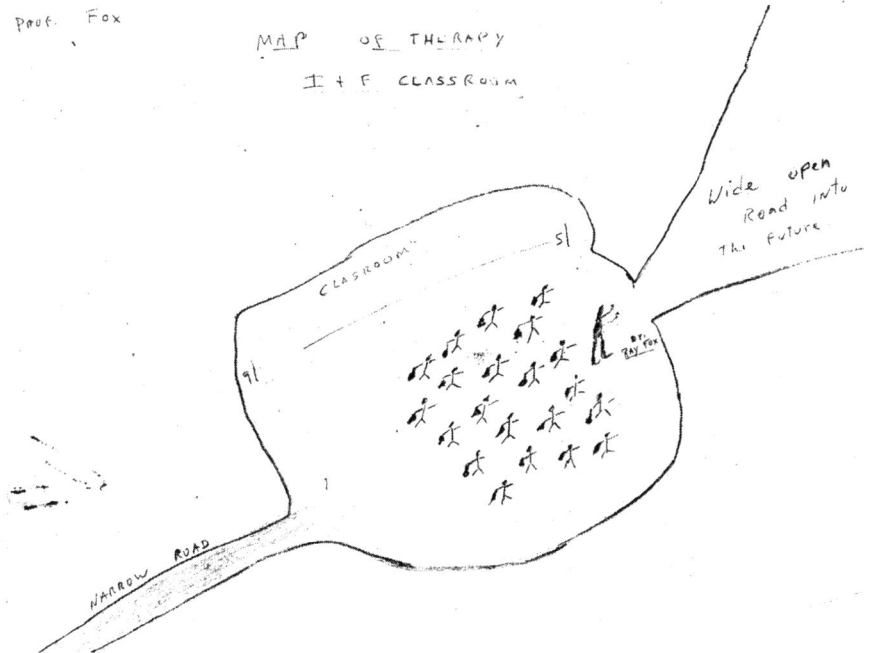

drawing connecting lines from their smaller circle to every other one, including the teacher, within the larger circle. Lines indicate a type of relationship
or communication existing among the class members: a straight line (—) represents a strong connection, a broken line (- - -) signifies a medium connection,
and an interrupted line (-|-|-|) connotes minimum or no connection.

In the second variation, to capture patterns of verbal interaction within
the class group, two volunteers are asked to be observers of the group as it
tackles a task or an issue. On a sheet of paper with a circle on it, they write
members' names in the order in which they are sitting. The observers are
instructed further to chart the interaction among the members by drawing an
arrow from the name of each speaker to each person spoken to. General
remarks not intended for a particular member are drawn to the middle of the
circle. Silent members stand out clearly.

Each of these "artworks" provides you and the members of the group
with a crystal-clear graphic of group dynamics as they unfold. They reveal
relationships, communication patterns, leadership positions, avoidances, and
so on. More important, they make immediate correction and refinement
possible.

THE JOHARI WINDOW

A more sophisticated framework, too elaborate to present in total here, is the
Johari Window, a graphic model of awareness in interpersonal relations
named for Joseph Luft and Harry Ingham (1963). The skeletal bare bones of
an adaptation of the model, aimed to clarify the functions of individual and
group feedback and self-disclosure, appears in table 9.

The first box (I) refers to behavior and motivation known to self and to
others.

The second box (II) refers to what others can see about ourselves of
which we are unaware.

The third box (III) refers to what we know about ourselves but do not
reveal to others.

The fourth box (IV) refers to what neither we nor others know.

A series of principles designates the use of the framework as change may
occur, with the main tenet being, change in any one quadrant affects the
others.

FINAL NOTE

In his novel, *The Bridges of Madison County* (1992), Robert James Waller has
the main character state, "When I'm finished with that bridge we saw today,

Table 9. The Johari Window

feedback

	Known to Self	Not Know to Self
Known to Others	I. The Public Self	II. The Blind Self
Not Known to Others	III. The Private Self	IV. The Unknown Area

exposure

it won't look quite like you expect. I'll have made it into something of my own, by lens choice, or camera angle, or general composition, and most likely by some combination of all of those. I don't just take things as given, I try to make them into something that reflects my personal consciousness, my spirit." So it is with photography and art as integral parts of your lessons.

As with other techniques discussed in the book, photography and art projects demand the brain's recruiting both hemispheres, right and left, to make sense of experience. The brain works by pattern recognition. It relies on memory and responds to images more quickly and fully than to words. When photography, artwork, images, and words are amalgamated in the teaching/learning process, they stretch the brain, making it elastic in its detection of themes, interpretation of metaphors, connection between images and words, and breakthrough in insight. These help as well in the interception of details and the big picture.

Role Playing

Suit the action to the word, the word to the action.

—HAMLET

Playing a role often provides an authentic way to learn truths about the real world. Suiting the action, as Hamlet says, by teaching with an experience simulation method such as role playing, effectively stimulates students toward their own learning.

Role plays make students sit up and take notice. A variant of or an adjunct to the case method, role plays arouse students' interest because they resemble real practice experiences.

Role players speak in the first person. Rather than commenting indirectly on what they think clients might say, they speak as if they actually were the clients. Key is having students immerse themselves in a realistic situation and then imagine themselves as the person in that situation. In other words, engage fully, intellectually and emotionally, in assuming a part in the play.

Effective role plays simulate reality as they stimulate learning. They support knowledge and skill attainment along the four axes identified by Kolb (1984)—concretely experiencing, observing and reflecting, abstract reasoning, and actively experimenting. At the same time, they involve learning by doing with the fundamental five-step, problem-solving paradigm proposed by Dewey—feeling a need, analyzing the difficulty, proposing alternative solutions, experimenting with various solutions, and applying the solutions to new and different settings. Role plays likewise meet Knowles' (1980) requisites for adult learning—empowering students to take responsibility for their own learning, drawing upon their unique experiences and strengths, making learning closely parallel practice, providing opportunities for students to reflect on their work, and engaging students in critical thinking.

A plastic and fluid method, role play constantly expands students' involvement and allows them to test knowledge and skill by repeated and rehearsed use. It subsequently has educational and practice relevance. By assuming various roles in a contrived yet nevertheless authentically represented situation, students reframe their understanding and develop alternative definitions of themselves and others. Role play therefore addresses four broad categories of professional practice objectives: it assists students to implement new information, sensitizes them to their own attitudes and beliefs, enlightens them to the motives and behaviors of others, and focuses on why.

Pretending taps both the right and left brain. It grasps information holistically, capitalizing on a series of sensory channels—speaking, moving, hearing, and seeing—as it provokes thoughtful consideration and analysis.

This chapter proposes process, procedure, preparation, performance, and post-review for drawing upon this make-believe strategy. Its impact on students' retention is far greater than simply reading from a book or hearing a lecture. Saying words, feeling emotions, and performing actions combine to make a powerful impression and sharpen communication skills. Role play enlivens remote and routine academic material.

WHY USE ROLE PLAY?

Detractors claim that role play is a poor substitute for the real thing. Indeed, it can be over-simplified and misleading, end up as frivolous, and exclude other sound methods of learning. Despite this criticism, many of its proponents applaud role play as an energizing and stimulating method. Certainly the effectiveness of the exercise is related to the ability of each student to imagine and portray a character; yet students are remarkably open to methods such as role play. Portrayal involves learning by doing, through imitation of desired behaviors, observation, feedback on performance (self, teacher/ practitioner, colleagues), reflection, analysis, and conceptualization and application of theoretical underpinnings. Think of elite athletes practicing moves and motions in labs far removed from the sports field in order to perfect their skills.

Students comment that role play allows them to see situations from alternative points of view; to practice a specific, demonstrable skill; to receive immediate corrective feedback; to exercise discretion; and even to try out approaches they would hesitate to attempt in real life. This all happens without any danger of harming a client. Added to these is the crucial benefit that emerges from examining one's own reactions. Role play bridges the gap between knowing something, feeling it, and actually doing it.

Demanding great involvement, role play transcends the players. It recruits peripheral observers in comprehending the association between what is enacted and relates to concepts and principles previously learned. Especially when students have little or no direct experience, such shared learning is inclusive and moves beyond mere spectatorship to engagement. The bonus for the players is having a host of others to learn from. The unique value of role playing lies chiefly in its simultaneity, spontaneity, and verisimilitude. Students assuming roles act holistically, not partially, since they undertake a self-generated reaction to the artificial situation. They feel, think, and behave as in real life.

CATEGORIES OF ROLE PLAY

There are a great variety of approaches to role play. These include formal structured, semi-structured, unstructured, or spontaneous. Role plays can be undertaken by individuals, groups, or in multiples. A role play can extend over a few minutes, or even over several class meetings. It also can also be videotaped for replay and examination. It can be employed as an auxiliary procedure, supplementing other methods such as storytelling (chapter 10), and case presentation (chapter 11). It can also be the primary technique for a lesson.

Consciously adopting and examining roles from your own practice, from literature, movies, or from student input requires different types of planning to make the activity relevant to the needs both of the curriculum and of the students. You need to decide whether students will be themselves or assume another identity. Either way, players will invariably supplement the role with personal voices.

Structured Role Play

Preparation is pivotal for structured role plays. They consume considerable time. Time is needed not only to acquaint students with details of the intended scenario, but to plan adequately for encompassing the stages inherent in its unfolding—outlining the roles, performing the roles, and processing the entire play. Formatted in advance with excerpts from textbooks, movies, or case records of students or your own, these role plays are generally scripted. They thereby allow you greater assurance that the play and its ensuing discussion of action, character, and context lead to a meaningful climax germane to the subject under study. It offers control. Role plays can be based on actual events or purely fictitious situations. Either way, all should be clarified at the outset.

Begin by ascertaining the learning goal. Prepare written information cards or handouts for the role players and, perhaps, the observers. The objectives should be given to the class in the form of guidelines for the role play. The students involved directly in the role play should be clear as to their roles, and the observers should be clear as to what they are looking for in the role play. The debriefing, feedback, postmortem evaluative process following the play will be more fruitful and comprehensive.

These handouts may include descriptions of players, the situation being enacted (initial interview, diagnostic, addiction, family, etc.), background scenario, and scope of the problem or issue. Establish a realistic time frame. Outline the rules for discussion and spell out the parameters for providing feedback. Other instructions may include a handout such as an interviewing skills inventory that the audience of observing students uses to provide feedback to the enactment. In this way, students can better analyze how well the simulation achieved its objectives, allowing you to make further commentary to link the role play to the topic under study. Be certain to make participation voluntary and provide ample time in advance for the students to familiarize themselves with the backgrounds of the roles and the state of affairs.

A schematic of steps in the process is shown in figure 7.

An example of a direction card from a foundation course clinical practice dealing with empathy reads:

> You will be divided into small groups of six to eight students. In pairs, you will be asked to involve yourself in the role plays scripted on the page provided. These will resemble situations that may occur in your internships. After a preparation period in which you will read your role, you will play that role before the small group. Choose a partner with whom you would like to work. Select roles from the list below and choose your own role, with your partner choosing a different one. Read role descriptions on the page provided. Meditate on your role and try to step into that person's shoes, empathizing with the feelings, thoughts, fears, and so on. Practice role reversals during several role-play repetitions to enable you to appreciate the other person's point of view. The group will comment on ways you demonstrated empathy.

The following role descriptions are drawn from a module in a subsequent class, emphasizing the task of conducting an initial interview. These are accompanied by an observation form for students to refer to as they form a circle around the players. The form, extrapolating concepts on assigned readings, guides discussion.

This format rests on the premise that performance is more successful when a skill is modeled first. Often students are reluctant initially to take on the role of clinician; therefore you might assume that role or serve as the auxiliary ego of the student to coach them. Eventually, as they become more confident and comfortable, students acquire the courage to play the clinician's role. Approximations and modeling are keys in shaping and refining skills, making them transferable to real practice outside the classroom. Before

Figure 7. The Effective Use of Role Play

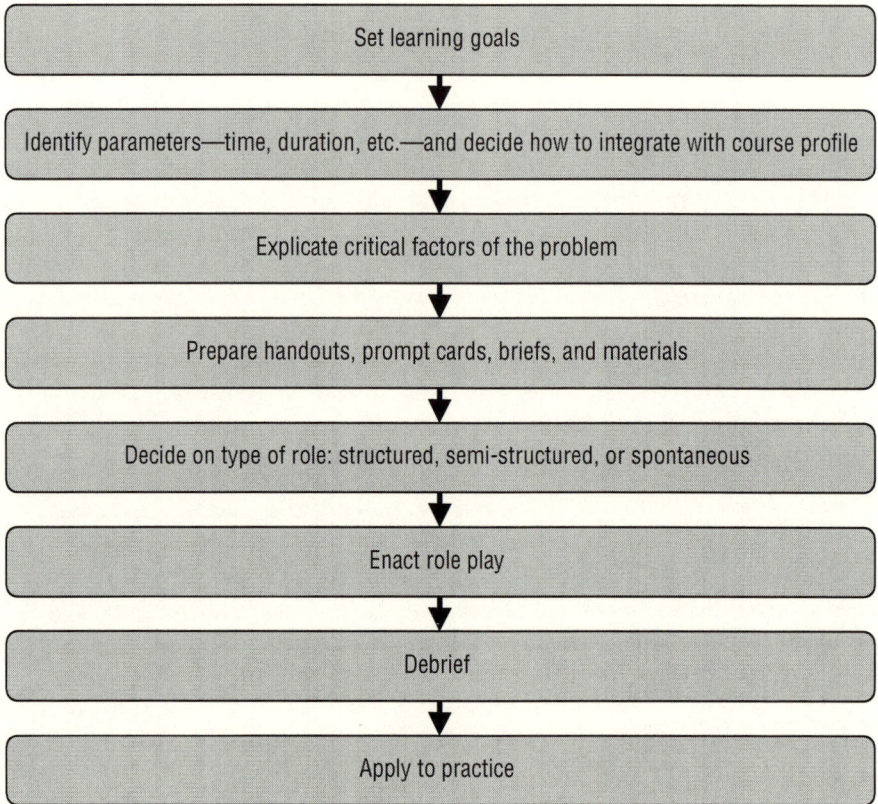

Set learning goals

↓

Identify parameters—time, duration, etc.—and decide how to integrate with course profile

↓

Explicate critical factors of the problem

↓

Prepare handouts, prompt cards, briefs, and materials

↓

Decide on type of role: structured, semi-structured, or spontaneous

↓

Enact role play

↓

Debrief

↓

Apply to practice

implementing skills in the natural setting, students have the opportunity to rehearse them in a protected atmosphere.

INFORMATION SHEET FOR THE CLINICIAN

Mr. J is a thirty-five-year-old white male, married for ten years, who works as a carpenter. Since the suicide three weeks ago of his father-in-law, who lived in Mr. J's house, Mr. J has been experiencing shortness of breath, sweaty palms, lack of concentration, and uncontrollable crying. These symptoms occur mostly at work. Mr. J fears that people at work will discover this and react negatively to him and that his lack of productivity will be seen and possibly cost him his job. He also fears that his lack of concentration could result in an accident since he works with power tools that require precision and vigilance. Mr. J has never been to therapy and appears apprehensive and uncertain about being involved.

INFORMATION SHEET FOR CLIENT (MR. J)

Mr. J is a thirty-five-year-old white male, married for ten years, who works as a carpenter. Since the suicide three weeks ago of his father-in-law, who lived in Mr. J's house, Mr. J has been experiencing shortness of breath, sweaty palms, lack of concentration, and uncontrollable crying. These symptoms occur mostly at work. Mr. J fears that people at work will discover this and react negatively to him and that his lack of productivity will be seen and possibly cost him his job. He also fears that his lack of concentration could result in an accident since he works with power tools that require precision and being vigilant. Mr. J reports that his wife's family is doing fine concerning the suicide. "That's the problem, I'm the only one who seems to be having a problem." Mr. J's wife's family has a history of drug and alcohol abuse. As a result, since his marriage various family members have lived with them. Mr. J's family members are supportive and actually have made the referral for professional help. Mr. J states that he is very close to his mother. His father has always been distant. He reports having received severe corporal punishment from his father because of his school performance. According to Mr. J, his parents tolerate his wife's family but stay away because of all the chaos. Mr. J has never been to therapy and appears apprehensive and uncertain about being involved.

Accompanying this scenario is the form, "Observation of First Interview Tasks" (see table 10), designed to break down the clinician's role into manageable parts.

At the exercise's conclusion, students can ask questions of you and of one another. They weigh the pros and cons of alternatives, try on positions different from their own. They respond favorably when their suggestions are taken seriously and when dissection and decision-making occur collegially.

Structured Role Play: From Student Assignments

In one graduate course in teaching, the overall final assignment requires students to deliver a lesson based on their previous midterm research into teaching methods. The catch for this oral presentation is that they must employ that particular method to teach the method. For example, if a student researches lecture, the oral presentation involves delivering a lecture on lecturing. If the topic is Socratic questioning, Socratic questioning becomes the dominant method to teach this method. One student based the final presentation on a combined individual and group role play. It entailed a panel of

Table 10. Observation of First Interview Tasks

Social Worker Basic Tasks	Comments
Explain purpose and role • obstacles to fulfilling purpose and role • authority issues	
Identify presenting problem (near problem)	
Give feedback re: presenting problem	
Gather basic assessment data • explain the why of the assessment	
Partialize problem	
Begin contracting process • who will do what	
Explain confidentiality	
Schedule next appointment	

famous educators proffering their philosophies of education. The week before the presentation, students were given this homework assignment:

> The profiles you have received relate to the lesson next Monday based on "role play." Each of you is being assigned a different famous educator who was a leader in shaping the professional educational process in history. Each one of these characters has greatly contributed in a highly regarded manner to the attitudes, philosophy, and values of the profession, specifically schooling for practice. An esteemed teacher, researcher, or independent thinker, this person occupies a special place in the history of professional education. The creative ability of this person has stimulated growth and quality of achievement in the past to help define the future.
>
> The goal of the lesson through role play will be to understand the basic views of the assigned educator, understand many different conceptual views, to learn about the history of professional education, and to place a theoretical perspective into process for helping to build tools for broadening and deepening our own knowledge base.
>
> By reading the assigned passage, you will begin to develop a basic understanding of the educator you will role play. You may supplement this summary with outside reading suggested on the appended bibliography. Next week you will *become* this person as you converse with students in their respective roles in a simulated roundtable discussion. It is important to know about your character thoroughly and intimately.

Each student was designated as a prominent educational theoretician. Each esteemed "expert," identified by a name tag, joined the panel to advance ideas representing their position, perspective, and approach to education. The panel conferred and argued the validity of their respective positions. And it happened! The role play's spirited exchange succeeded in bringing abstract concepts to life.

Structured role plays cover theoretical ground in a way that makes practical sense but also constitutes a spirited exchange. Role playing brings concepts to life.

Semi-Structured Role Play

In semi-structured role plays, specifics are not as clearly or finely delineated as they are with structured ones. By and large, the genesis of these are your own or students' own case material, which may naturally lend itself to functional staging.

It's possible to take professionally prepared videotapes of experts doing therapy a step beyond simply viewing them. For example, one creative use of canned videos is showing students only an introductory segment of a tape providing background data and characterization. Students then undertake roles represented in the tape. Inventing interventions and next steps, they portray possible ways to approach the issues depicted. After this role play and its examination, resume showing the next segment of the tape with the expert. Reconsideration of the role play in light of its contrast with the expert's action results in fruitful discussion of similarities, alternatives, and differences in technique, dynamics, foci, and the application of theoretical knowledge. Requiring less prior preparation than does a structured role play, it nevertheless necessitates careful selection of the targeted episode to assure its appropriateness. Such attention is essential to assure that the objective of the lesson is met since the role play, without such forethought, may stray in unanticipated directions.

Classes often begin with students presenting issues they face in their internships. They seek guidance and direction as to how to proceed. Quick to discuss a firsthand account of their experience, these accounts often evolve into role plays as when Ruth described the following:

> My first two sessions with Amy went okay. They were uneventful. The last one, the second one, she mainly spoke about her very strict, unaffectionate parents, particularly her mother. She did not show for her scheduled appointment last week, but has unexpectedly, and without explanation, reappeared today. I think she has potential, is somewhat insightful, and I'd like to continue to work with her. The trouble is, I also need her to stay in treatment because my supervisor has told me that my case load is dropping. I want to reengage her, and I'm not sure how to proceed.

Ruth agreed to play her client, another student played Ruth. After the role-playing, the class was divided into four groups. Each group imagined its being a panel of distinguished practitioners (a role play within a role play) invited to consult on the case. Their charge was to arrive at strategies to reengage Amy in treatment. How should Ruth proceed? How can she contract with Amy to continue? What are some suggestions? If she were to redo the interview, what might be different? How can Ruth support Amy's strengths? What should she avoid? Based on the commentary from the groups, Ruth accessed an array of practical avenues on which to proceed.

Spontaneous Role Play

Spontaneous role plays are improvised skits that flow naturally from classroom interaction. They require vigilance, as they are not scripted in advance and therefore somewhat unpredictable. They are, however, often inspired vehicles for producing reflection-in-action (Schon, 1983, 1987).

At the beginning of a semester, as is typical in most classrooms, students are asked their names and their goal for the course. At times, I will stop and request students to elaborate on their names. Asking if they mind pursuing this track, I grab a chair and sit nearby as we speak. Not exactly a role play, it tacitly depicts for students a way to undertake a non-threatening first interview. Afterward the class is asked to identify what has been gleaned from this conversation, an ordinary conversation about a name. They are astounded at the amount of information that flows from simple inquiry. Among the lessons gleaned—about proximity boundaries, touching, guarding against too rapid or intense an intrusion early in professional work—is the key one: you can garner compelling information from such non-intrusive inquiry.

In another instance—again, not quite a true role play—I take off my shoes without explanation to exhibit the maxim about walking a mile in someone else's shoes. A student is invited to step into them and walk. The exercise leads not only to class insights, but often to epiphanies—such as the observation that it is necessary for a practitioner to step into the client's shoes, but most imperative for them is to get out of them and back into their own in order to effect change.

A dramatic role play can emerge from co-constructing a fictional case. Students propose data—concrete demographic information, presenting problems and issues, attendant inferences and speculations, and possible interventions. The information is itemized and collectively categorized into a framework written on the blackboard for further analysis. When contributions slow down or cease, you may query for further ideas, recommendations, and refinements. As students reflect on this fictional case, the process elicits an uncanny correspondence to their present practice. They say things ranging from the interpersonal ("It looks just like a situation I have at the office") to the impersonal ("It seems very complicated") to the practical ("So that's a good way to tackle a case like that?"). Each time this venture takes place, it is uniquely formulated and constructed. Students are enthusiastic about the exercise because they supply the basic information, which they themselves transform into a lively enactment.

Whether structured, semi-structured, or spontaneous, keep in mind that preparation and debriefing are as critical as the portrayal.

On-the-spot role plays can be extremely compelling; however, consider some precautions. Because of its voluntary and momentary nature, emotionally laden personal material may spill over into the exercise. Remember that a class, however moving, is no substitute for therapy. When charged emotional material surfaces, address it without exploring it in depth, and identify appropriate resources.

While playing the role of a practitioner conducting a suicide assessment in one class, for example, a student more than hinted at its pertinence to him. It was necessary to gently interrupt and stop the role play. I spoke didactically about process and asked him to confer with me privately in my office after class. He followed up this conversation with making an appointment with the university counselor.

Be on your toes to handle surprises cropping up during spontaneous role plays, such as reticence, resistance, and confusion.

PREPARATION

Warm up is essential no matter which direction you take. Anticipate constraints and barriers to increase the emergence of an effective role play. Be sure to explain the process in general as well as acquaint students with the particular instance. Take care in selecting participants. Set the stage. Prepare players and observers alike. Provide specific instructions and directions, that is, train the class how to observe. Consider in advance when you plan to interrupt the action, when to conclude, and how to keep things on track. Let the following questions guide you in whether to introduce a role play in or class or not: Is role play the best method of choice? Can these particular students enter easily into the role play? Will the selected scene or dilemma reflect the focus under study? How can the portrayal be structured? What is the best format? Will it arouse a lively interchange of ideas? Are the details straightforward enough to permit dramatic enactment?

Before launching into a role play, it is helpful to undertake a variation of a force field analysis to unpack its details. Lewin's (1969) theory that what appears to be stability in situations is actually opposing forces in a state of equilibrium and involves driving and restraining forces. Changing the status quo demands unbalancing the forces. Component forces can be modified by reducing or removing forces, strengthening or adding forces, or changing the direction of the forces. Decisions revolve around what kind of change is desired (e.g., attitudinal, behavioral, structural), what factor(s) warrant change (e.g., individual, group, family, organizational, policy), and what direction should be taken in rebalancing opposing forces. Lewin indicated that removing the restraining forces is probably the most effective method because increasing a driving force usually results in increasing a restraining force. Alternative strategies, however, should be taken into cognizance. The schematic outline on the board, following the pattern below, takes shape as students identify the relevant data, listing factors that facilitate or hinder the situation. Those factors fall into two categories, each further subdivided, from which a plan emerges as to which forces may be acted on in the role play. After rating the influence of each force as it pertains to the situation, and keeping uppermost in mind how the situation looks *now* versus the way it will look *afterward*, the role play commences. The template for setting up the role play from a force field reference point appears in figure 8.

This adaptation of the force field design for the purpose of running a role play, actually embeds a conceptual lesson in and of itself about force field theory and planning.

DEBRIEFING

Post-enactment analysis is critical. It has many purposes: drawing inferences and conclusions from the rendering; clarifying misunderstandings; deducing principles; challenging previous ways of thinking ("we've always done it that way"); addressing reservations; and providing feedback that is respectful, positive, timely, accurate, helpful, and usable.

Orchestrate the debriefing to closely follow the role play. Immediately after is best. To begin, bring role play to closure by having the role players reflect on their own feelings, difficulties, learnings. Provide sufficient time for them to share their self-observations. Have observers report or summarize what they saw or what they noted, how they can relate it to their knowledge. Encourage them as well to offer subjective reactions to what transpired. Link the role play to the stated objectives of that particular class or module, and to the course in general in terms of its assimilation of new knowledge and introduction of new skills. This link facilitates students' applying their learning to authentic practice situations. Future learning goals can also be discussed at this time.

Debriefing is more than a cooling off period and a readjustment to the routine conduct of the class. It crystallizes learning and can be as powerful as the role play itself.

Guidelines for feedback protect players from overexposure to negative remarks. Advocate remaining tentative and in the here and now. Recommend

Figure 8. Situation at Present

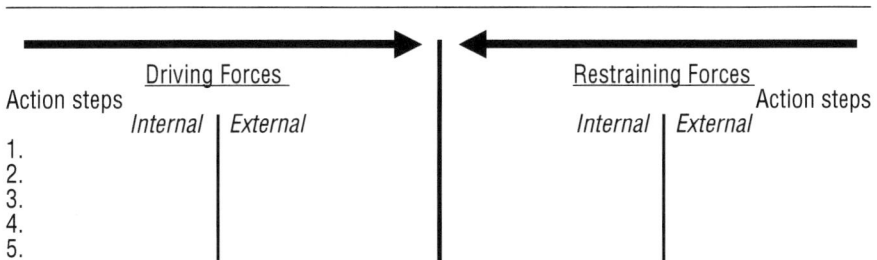

Driving Forces		Restraining Forces	
Action steps			Action steps
Internal	*External*	*Internal*	*External*
1.			
2.			
3.			
4.			
5.			

raising a smorgasbord of ideas, using specific rather than general words and abstract comments, underscoring strengths, suggesting possible alternatives, recommending improvements, and avoiding advice or judgment—all attributes of dialogue with clients. *Feedback* is transformed into an acronym and distributed as a handout, as follows:

F ocuses on what is changeable, descriptive, specific
E xtends and shares parts of each of you
E licits feelings, reactions, suggestions, and questions
D escribes rather than confines, judges, or interprets
B uilds on honesty and openness
A llows time and space for thorough consideration
C oncentrates on and reinforces observable changes
K nits secure relationships

UTILIZATION VARIATION

There are a number of ways to develop and enrich a role play. A few have been alluded to earlier, such as reenactment based on feedback, rotating between a prepared case or movie and a role play, and freezing the action. I tend to avoid multiple role plays, finding it impossible to observe all of them at once, give them equitable attention, and provide plausible feedback in a timely and logical fashion. Adopting or adapting techniques from individual and family therapy can augment role playing. Briefly described, they hint at supplemental ways to undertake or assess role plays. Introducing them also serves to introduce students to thumbnail sketches or mini-lessons of practice approaches that are not encompassed fully in the course.

- Having an *alter ego* to assist in the role play. This double coaches the role player to remain faithful to the role, offer direction when the player is stuck, and recommend a different style of communicating.
- *Role reversal* involves you and students, and students and students, alternately switching positions and conferring on the enactment.
- *Role rotation* takes place when a series of different students replay an identical situation in a variety of ways, demonstrating different styles and strategies.
- A *fishbowl* is composed of an inner group of students seated in a circle, performing a role play or some combination of you and students undertaking a task witnessed by a larger group that provides input in terms of patterns, themes, different points of view about aspects of the portrayal of issues or problems. It allows students to practice skills while being observed by others who critique the performance in a supportive way,

thus increasing understanding of perspectives about issues and interventions and linking ideas that may have been hidden. It makes the larger outside group feel that their viewpoints are represented even when they have not themselves directly dealt with the task at hand. Participants and observers leave the fishbowl with a greater understanding of the range of opinions and experiences that obtain. Be sure to balance the activity between the students within the fishbowl and the observers.

- *Greek chorus* is a form of fishbowl. However, whereas the fishbowl design commentary *follows* the role play, in the Greek chorus, commentary is *ongoing* throughout the role play. Messages of support, advice, and disagreement are relayed directly to the inner circle of role players as they perform the enactment, immediately shifting the interchange. While in the family therapy, the consultants are invisible and their remarks non-negotiable, the classroom experience is more public.

- *Sculpting* is another method from family treatment. With its roots in psychodrama, it is a nonverbal, non-interpretative technique that telescopes and freeze-frames the class's critical moments and reactions into physical positions. The teacher, student, or a combination of students physically mold targeted students themselves or even the teacher, so that their assumed postures and spatial relationships represent impressions and interpretations that words alone cannot provide.

  Sculptors translate their perceptions into a visual image conveyed visually through a tangible and poignant sculpture. This sensory arrangement physically symbolizes elusive, thorny, and intricate thoughts and feelings, often lost when verbalized, cutting through excessive intellectualization.

- The *hot seat*, or *empty chair*, technique from Gestalt therapy is informative and constructive when used in the classroom. When students express difficulty entering the exercise, ask them to experiment with a different form of role play where their difficulty is imagined as sitting in an empty chair across from them. Switching chairs, they become the difficulty and respond to themselves occupying the original, now vacant, chair. This role play helps them through self-discovery to experience and understand their reservation more fully and move past it onto the intended role play. Innumerable options are possible for conducting this dialogue with self—other people, parts of personality, stereotypes. This dialogue clarifies feelings and reactions.

- *Videotaping* students' role plays is invaluable to tweak skills and to recognize theory as it bears on practice. Rewinding portions of a recorded role play, watching segments over and over, pausing to highlight selected episodes, fast forwarding it to see end results of particular actions, and returning to it at other times during that class or later in the course cultivates stunning insights. Reenacting the role play, taping it again, and comparing and contrasting the two versions further augments learning.

Epilogue

Preach always and sometimes use words.

—ST. FRANCIS OF ASSISI

This quotation highlights the decisive role of teachers in laying the foundation by their example for students to learn to become professional practitioners. Teachers demonstrate in their demeanor the intellectual, affective, and ethical bases of their expertise.

Many see faculty as remote figures lecturing behind a rostrum with the expectation that students passively memorize facts and jargon. *The Use of Self* proposes instead a more active, learner-centered process, one in which the foremost signatures of professional education are relationship and reflection. Here students have the opportunity to discuss, argue, inquire, integrate, and apply knowledge and skill in larger thematic patterns. It suggests that the finest teachers certainly render precise theories and research findings at the cognitive level. More significant, however, they make students feel heard, understood, and cared about on the emotional plane. They marry the rational with the sensitive, the science with the art, the head with the heart, making a direct connection between formal knowledge and the uncertainties or ambiguities of practice.

In this framework, relationship and reflection share a symbiotic connection to learning. As the depth and breadth of relationship expands, so too will the depth and breadth of reflection, and ultimately that of learning and understanding. Mere information is not knowledge. To be transformed into knowledge, information needs to shift to higher levels of cognitive and affective discrimination through experiential challenges linking content to practice.

Beyond providing what students need to know conceptually, teachers, by creating an environment conducive to honest, intensive, and meaningful interaction, provide these most essential elements to professional education and practice. *The Use of Self* is based on a fundamental principle—a teachers' relationship and ongoing reflection with students most strongly influences students' learning to work with clients. While teachers do not practice on their students, their deportment bears a unique resemblance to the basic ingredients of help-giving. The methods they undertake with students—contracting, responding, questioning, and so on—parallel those students learn to deliver to clients. This process is stimulated through dialogue and arises from the cognitive and affective synthesis of shared perspectives and the meanings ascribed to them.

This book concentrates on the rudiments of the professional encounter. It proposes that methods the teacher chooses to instruct should be substantively similar to the ones that students are encouraged to employ with clients. Relationship-building is key. It has multiple purposes: establishing and sustaining an atmosphere that reduces learners' anxieties and defensiveness; creating pathways for open and mutual exchange; forming a context of safety; and, most important of all, providing a paradigm for students to draw upon in formulating their own professional and practice stance.

How to respond to clients suffering from the absence of secure human relationships is learned in a forum that itself provides a steady, trustworthy, and consistent milieu—a safe classroom. Students achieve the capacity for learning from experience and effective and independent functioning through the cardinal intertwined processes of *modeling, mirroring,* and *mentoring* combined with continual *reflection.*

Reflection is profoundly influenced by an examination of ongoing interactions between teachers and students. As a class unfolds, effective teachers explicitly inform students of their instructional decisions and underlying theories supporting those decisions. They invite students' deliberations about alternative interpretations of what transpires in the classroom. They endeavor to convert into concrete and lucid terms what automatically and intuitively feels right. Through such intellectual and affective exchange, students and teachers explore their experiences in order to construct meaningful understandings and relevant practice.

Reflection is a product of experience combined with example. It relies on employing various experiential techniques, including those from popular culture that foster deepened contemplation. This book expounds upon six well-tested, creative, and interdependent strategies with illustrative examples to advance and enrich relational acuity and reflective discernment. These are: introspective *journaling*, thought-provoking *movies*, poignant *stories*, down-to-earth *case/critical incidents*, analogic *photography and art*, and realistic *role playing.*

The Use of Self advances the idea that professional pursuits at every level involve a deliberate, conscious, and disciplined use of self. A teacher's and a practitioner's personhood is the predominant medium of rapport-building and transmission. Teachers play a direct role in developing students' professional character by designing lessons in ways that translate the abstract and philosophical into deliverable subject matter. It requires a keen grasp of how best to use your self. It entails familiarity with students' varying learning styles along with adaptation of your own style so as best to appeal to students' strengths.

Overall, the essence of education for the profession rests on the exquisite interface between teaching and practicing. The knowledge, skill, and value base of both intersect and propel one another. Teaching influences practice principally by example. Practice informs teaching largely by exposition. Critical reflection upon their current respective beliefs and practices by both teachers and students develops the habits and skills necessary for self-directed growth and prepares them to participate as full-fledged contributors to the community of caregivers.

References

Bettelheim, B. (1976). *The uses of enchantment: The meaning and importance of fairy tales*. New York: Knopf.

Bruner, J. (1996). *The culture of education*. Cambridge, MA: Harvard University Press.

Campbell, J. (1988). *The power of myth*. New York: Doubleday.

Carey, M., Fox, R., & Penney, J. (2002). *The artful journal: A spiritual quest*. New York: Watson-Guptill.

Coles, R. (1989). *The call of stories: Teaching and the moral imagination*. Boston: Houghton Mifflin.

Dewey, J. (1933). *How we think: A restatement of the relation of reflective thinking to the educative process*. New York: DC Heath and Company.

Dewey, J. (1938). *Logic, the Theory of Inquiry*. New York: Henry Holt and Co.

Dewey, J. (1974). *On education: Selected writings*. Chicago: University of Chicago Press.

Erikson, E. (1950). *Childhood and society*. New York: W. W. Norton.

Estes, C. P. (1992). *Women who run with wolves and stories of the wild woman archetype*. New York: Ballantine Books.

Fox, R. (2001). *Elements of the helping process: A guide for clinicians*. Binghamton, NY: Haworth Press.

Fox, R., & Gutheil, I. (2000). Process recording: A means for conceptualizing and evaluating practice. *Journal of Teaching in Social Work*, *20*(1/2), 39–56.

Freire, P. (1970). *Pedagogy of the oppressed*. New York: Seabury.

Gardner, H. (1983). *Frames of mind: The theory of multiple intelligences*. New York: Basic Books.

Gardner, H. (2007). *Five minds for the future*. Boston: Harvard Business School Press.

Jung, C. G. (1954). *The portable Jung: The collected works of C. G. Jung*. New York: Penguin Books.

Jung, C. G. (1971). *The collected works of C. G. Jung,* vol. 6: *Psychological types*. (R. F. C. Hull, Ed.). Princeton, NJ: Princeton University Press.

Knowles, M. (1980). *The modern practice of adult education*. Chicago: Follet.

Knowles, M. (1984). *Andragogy in action: Applying modern principles of adult learning*. San Francisco: Jossey-Bass.

Kohut, H. (1977). *The Restoration of the self*. New York: International Universities Press.

Kolb, D. (1984). *Experiential learning: Experience as the source of learning.* New York: Prentice-Hall.

Laird, J. (1989). *Women and stories: Restorying women's self-constructions.* New York: W. W. Norton.

Lewin, K. (1969). Quasi-stationary social equilibria and the problem of permanent changes. In W. G. Bennis, K. D. Benne, & R. Chin (Eds.) *The planning of change* (pp. 73–78). New York: Holt, Rinehart, and Winston.

Luft, J., & Ingham, H. (1963). *Group processes: An introduction to group dynamics* (3rd ed.). Mountain View, CA: Mayfield Pub. Co.

Myers, I. B. (1976). *The Myers-Briggs Type Indicator: Supplementary manual.* Palo Alto, CA: Consulting Psychologists Press.

Ravazzin Center for Social Work Research in Aging. (2003). *Generalist Social Work Practice with Individuals, Families, and Groups I: Teaching Casebook.* New York: Ravazzin Center Publications (Fordham University).

Rico, G. L. (1983). *Writing the natural way.* Los Angeles: J. P. Tarcher, Inc.

Rogers, C. (1958). The characteristics of a helping relationship. *Personnel and Guidance Journal, 3*(1), 383–391.

Rogers, C. (1961). *On becoming a person: A therapist's view of psychotherapy.* Boston: Houghton-Mifflin.

Rogers, C. (1980). *A way of being.* Boston: Houghton Mifflin Company.

Rogers, C. (1983). *Freedom to learn in the '80s.* Columbus, OH: Charles E. Merrill.

Schon, D. (1983). *The reflective practitioner: How professionals think in action.* London: Temple Smith.

Schon, D. (1987). *Educating the reflective practitioner: Toward a new design for teaching and learning in the professions.* San Francisco: Jossey-Bass Publishers.

Setterfield, D. (2007). *The thirteenth tale.* New York: Washington Square Press.

Sontag, S. (1977). *On photography.* New York: Farrar, Straus, and Giroux.

Sontag. S. (2004, May 23). Regarding the torture of others. *New York Times Magazine,* p. 25.

Tompkins, J. (1996) *A life in school: What the teacher learned.* Cambridge, MA: Perseus Books.

Towle, C. (1945). *Common human needs.* Washington, DC: Federal Security Agency.

Towle, C. (1954). *The learner in education for the professions: As seen in education for social work.* Chicago: University of Chicago Press.

Waller, R. J. (1992) *The Bridges of Madison County.* New York: Warner Books.

Winnicott, D. W. (1971). *Playing and reality.* New York: Basic Books.

Index

About the Author

Raymond Fox (PhD; LCSW), professor at Fordham University Graduate School of Social Service, teaches master and doctoral courses in clinical practice, professional education, and philosophy of science. Having maintained a private practice as a certified individual, family, sex, and group psychotherapist, he has supervised therapists in these areas and served as a training and organizational consultant to an array of national and international mental health, family, and child welfare organizations. He developed and directed a postgraduate program in family therapy.

Fox has written several books and more than sixty book chapters and journal articles that focus on journaling, clinical diagnosis and intervention, and teaching, including the first and second editions of *Elements of the Helping Process: A Guide for Clinicians* (1993; 2001) and (coauthor) *The Artful Journal: A Spiritual Quest* (2002). He is currently preparing the third edition of *Elements* and a book concentrating on movies to improve personal relationships.

For more than fifteen years he has conducted seminars and workshops for college and graduate school faculties dealing with teaching philosophy, processes, and creative strategies in higher education. He has received numerous awards for his teaching.